The Humanness of John Calvin

The Humanness of John Calvin

Richard Stauffer

Translated by

George H. Shriver

Abingdon Press

Nashville   New York

THE HUMANNESS OF JOHN CALVIN

ISBN 0-687-18033-3

Library of Congress Catalog Card Number: 79-148070

SET UP, PRINTED, AND BOUND BY THE
PARTHENON PRESS, AT NASHVILLE,
TENNESSEE, UNITED STATES OF AMERICA

To My Father
On His 70th Birthday
March 6, 1964

Foreword
by John T. McNeill

I have been honored by an invitation from the translator and the publisher, to write a foreword to this informing little book. The author, my esteemed friend, having graciously concurred, I gladly accept the assignment. I am particularly happy in the recollection that both the author and the translator have participated in seminars on Calvin that I conducted, the former as a graduate student in Union Theological Seminary, New York, in 1952, the latter as a visiting scholar in Duke University Divinity School in 1970. Richard Stauffer, when I first knew him a scholarly Swiss pastor, has rapidly reached high rank among church historians. He is a professor in both the Faculté de théologie protestante and in the Ecole des Hautes Etudes (Sorbonne), Paris. A highly productive scholar, he has published intensive studies of the seventeenth-century authors, Moïse Amyrault and Isaac D'Huisseau, certain articles on Luther, followed by an examination in book form of Roman Catholic judgments of the Saxon Reformer since 1904, entitled in its English edition *Luther as Seen by*

The Humanness of John Calvin

Catholics; a short account of the Reformation in the Que-sais-je? series, and a number of perceptive essays in interpretation of works of Calvin. He is a member of the group of Calvin experts engaged in editing the extensive series of *Supplementa* now being added to the *Calvina opera*, erroneously designated *"omnia."* Still within the younger class of qualified Reformation historians, Professor Stauffer is bound to be increasingly influential among students of that era. Happily for the present distinguished volume, a competent translator volunteered his services. Professor George H. Shriver, no novice either in Calvin study or as a translator of French, has, I believe, well captured the lucid and sprightly style of the original.

The book is one much needed, designed to disabuse the modern mind of a gross and persistent historical misjudgment. The attempt to reveal the true image of Calvin is not of course something new. Many of his biographers have incidentally defended him against misrepresentation. Notably, Emile Doumergue, Calvin scholar of immense learning, in 1921 put forth a small volume entitled *Le caractère de Calvin*, a study now out of date in its references and unprocurable. If Doumergue's admiration for Calvin is somewhat extreme, it grew out of a basis of facts that could not be gainsaid. In the decades between Doumergue and Stauffer a greatly increased attention to Calvin's writings has disposed the learned world to a more favorable view of his thought and personality. But he has been subjected anew to insidious attacks, samples of which are critically examined by Professor Stauffer in his introductory chapter. The attacks come from persons of different church affiliations, or of none. Unexamined, they tend to revive and perpetuate a false image of the Genevan Reformer as the satanic villain of his century.

Not only does Stauffer disperse the hate-laden legendary material about Calvin and the perverse judgments of some contemporary assailants, he also displays accumulated evidence of Calvin's quality of life as a Christian human being. Nobody can safely generalize on the real Calvin without knowledge of such revealing data as we find in abundance here regarding his home, his friendships, and his pastoral ministry. It will be noted that our author draws largely from the letters, a rich source too little explored. There is much of interest in this material for all readers, whatever presuppositions they may bring.

Some decades ago, when I began to acquaint myself with Calvin's writings, I soon felt obliged to abandon a set of uninformed prejudgments about him such as many students glean without effort from tradition and hearsay. He had been for me, not indeed the ogre he has sometimes appeared, but an alien historical figure for whom I had little sympathy or tolerance. But to read at large in his letters and treatises was to encounter multiple proofs of a vivid humanness, an outgoing concern for others and enjoyment of association with many of differing social rank, a gentle courtesy with correspondents, and a sturdy loyalty to friends, of whom in youth and age he had a wide circle. This aspect of his personality has been too little regarded, even by many who are familiar with the outlines of his theology. The warmth of his normal relations with his associates; his tenderness toward sufferers from pain or bereavement; his solicitous concern for the members of his correspondents' families; the generous hospitality of his home; his deep and lasting affection for his wife and appreciation of her fine qualities; his resolute commitment to a charitable course in church reform whereby small issues might not become occasions of alienation; his abiding sense of the communion of saints and of the brotherhood of man; these are amply attested elements of his personality which the blots upon his record should not be allowed to eclipse.

Those who have some acquaintance with the Calvin corpus will not be surprised by Stauffer's materials, but will be grateful for his succinct and convenient presentation of much information never similarly assembled before. For those who have been led to judge the Reformer by what they know of incidents in which he exhibited a strain of harsh intolerance, this book will open a new vista. Calvin has been so industriously defamed that many on the fringe of the educated world think of him primarily with a certain abhorrence. This is because he, like most of his contemporaries, approved, and in one or two instances sought, the death penalty for persistent heretics. Not long ago, in a university circle, I was introduced to a lady who had learned that I had some interest in Calvin. She at once remarked: "O yes, he was the one who burnt Servetius!" (*sic*). It is usually forgotten in this context that Calvin, alone of all who were involved in the Servetus case, made a plea for a more merciful form of execution. But the mention of his name evokes in many minds a picture of the lurid flames of Champel hill, while the innumerable scenes of similar burnings elsewhere, even in Calvin's days, are consigned to oblivion. It is not to be denied that Calvin was terribly wrong to approve execution for unorthodox belief. But we too would be quite wrong to deny him credit for the wide range of gracious and beneficent acts and counsels that characterized his daily life. As late as 1966, the Cambridge scholar Basil Hall noted that references to Calvin in unscholarly literature continue to be prevailingly pejorative and little related to what scholars have learned of him.[1] Such an attitude will

[1] In his essay "The Calvin Legend," in *Studies in John Calvin*, Courtenay Series on Reformation Theology, Vol. I, ed. G. E. Duffield (London and Grand Rapids, 1966), pp. 10 ff.

have to be abandoned by those who give a fair reading to this book.

It may be added that no uncritical adulation of Calvin is expressed or intended. When his admiring fellow workers of the Genevan church gathered tearfully to hear his words of farewell, he confessed: "I have had many faults that you have had to endure, and all that I have done is of no value." A similar self-disparagement at the end is attributed to the great Aquinas. Great men would be less great if they were not aware of their own defects and limitations. Contrary to some opinions, Calvin never imagined himself either an infallible theologian or a model of all saintly virtues. But he gave abundant proof of total dedication to the reform and renewal of the Christian church, and to this task he brought surpassing talents and sustained energy. Writing constantly on topics in controversy, wrestling with the problems of churches and nations and of persons in trouble, deeply involved in the life of his age, he was by some heartily opposed, hated, and maligned, by others, gratefully admired and beloved. As a figure of large significance in history Calvin should be known to us in the full dimension of his personality. Professor Stauffer's succinct chapters lead us a long way toward this result, and should be welcomed by a wide English-reading public.

Translator's Note

In the spring semester, 1970, it was a rare privilege and pleasure for me to attend many of the seminar sessions on John Calvin which were being directed by Professor John T. McNeill as Visiting Professor of Church History at Duke University Divinity School. It was he who first made me acquainted with the present volume. My first reading convinced me that it was worthy of translation. It is solidly based on the primary sources (especially the letters of Calvin) and exposes its readers to a dimension of Calvin's life and work which is often unknown or ignored. Richard Stauffer paints this part of the portrait so winsomely and appealingly! For the first time in my own brief career, I was convinced by this volume that John Calvin was really a member of the human race, that he had genuine "humanness." I commend the work to this end for other readers.

Professor McNeill gave the first encouragement and the last assistance in relation to this translation. Through his kindness and promptness in reading the translation, it has been improved at many points. For his yeoman's work I extend my deep appreciation. Indeed, whatever errors remain are the translator's. I can only hope that this translation at least does partial justice to Professor Stauffer's unique contribution and his beautiful French. Finally, my wife, Donna Newcomer Shriver, was a faithful typist and warm critic, and is thanked for undertaking these two difficult roles.

GEORGE H. SHRIVER

Wake Forest, North Carolina

Preface

Having already been translated into German, my book *The Humanness of John Calvin* is now made available to the English reader. I am especially pleased to thank my fellow professor Dr. George H. Shriver, professor of church history at Southeastern Baptist Theological Seminary, who has made an excellent translation of the work, and my esteemed teacher Dr. John T. McNeill, Professor Emeritus of Union Theological Seminary, to whom I owe, in addition to the favorable and kind preface which introduces this English edition, my very vocation as a historian of the Reformation (actually, while pursuing my studies at Union Theological Seminary in the academic year 1952-53, my eyes were opened to the interest and richness of the sixteenth century by Dr. McNeill's courses).

On the occasion of the appearance of this English edition, I would like to share a hope and a memory. The hope: that the portrait of Calvin as husband and father, friend and pastor, which I have tried to paint on these pages, might show to more than one reader the true stature of the Genevan

The Humanness of John Calvin

Reformer, who is also one of the spiritual fathers of the found-
ers of the United States. The memory: when I was a student
in New York and assisted in worship in the small French
Church of the Holy Spirit, I never failed to be moved upon
reading on the walls of the sanctuary the names of Huguenot
families which had found refuge in the New World. At that
time I could not help thinking (and it is still my belief to this
day) that these witnesses of the faith, uncompromising in
their convictions, were fully the descendants of this John Calvin, who, though human in his obedience, yet offered his
"heart as a burnt sacrifice to the Lord." It is in thinking of
these refugees of other years that I dedicate this essay, which
attempts to exonerate the name of Calvin, to contemporary
Americans who are mindful of their origins.

This work is the result of two lectures. One was given in
the Church of the Oratory in Paris, May 21, 1964, and the
second at the University of Basel, May 27, 1964, on the four
hundredth anniversary of the death of Calvin.

I have not intended to paint a complete portrait of the
Reformer. I have only hoped to spotlight several ignored
sides of his personality, allowing him to speak as much as
possible.

RICHARD STAUFFER

Contents

Abbreviations

O.C.	*Ioannis Calvini opera quae supersunt omnia,* edited by Guillaume Baum, Edouard Cunitz, and Edouard Reuss, 59 volumes, Brunswick and Berlin, 1863–1900.
O. S.	*Ioannis Calvini opera selecta,* edited by Peter Barth and Wilhelm Niesel, 5 volumes, Munich, 1926–1952.
Opuscules	*Recueil des opuscules, c'est-à-dire petits traités de M. Jean Calvin,* Geneva, 1566.
Comm. Ps.	*Commentaires de Jean Calvin sur le livre des Psaumes,* 2 volumes, Paris, 1859.
Comm. N.T.	*Commentaires de Jean Calvin sur le Nouveau Testament,* 4 volumes, Paris, 1854–1855.
Bonnet	*Lettres de Jean Calvin recueillies pour la première fois et publiées d'après les manuscrits originaux,* by Jules Bonnet, 2 volumes, Paris, 1854.
Herminjard	*Correspondance des Réformateurs dans les pays de langue française* (1512-1544), collected and published by A.-L. Herminjard, 9 volumes, Geneva and Paris, 1866–1897.
BSHPF	*Bulletin de la Société de l'histoire du protestantisme français,* Paris, 1853 ss.

Introduction

Through the course of four centuries, the reformers have been exposed to critiques as varied as they have been severe. Among them, however, there is not one who has been more bitterly discussed than Calvin.[1] Luther, by his spontaneity and his exuberant spirit, even succeeded in awakening sympathy from his very opponents,[2] and Zwingli commanded respect as a lucid patriot and a courageous soldier in the very ones who would contest his theology, but the French reformer not only has suffered calumny from his enemies, he has also been misunderstood and misinterpreted by his great-grandchildren.[3]

[1] It is not meaningless that Peter Vogelsanger entitled the first paragraph of the article in which he dealt with Calvin on the occasion of the 1959 celebration, "Der Vielgeschmähte" (cf. "Johannes Calvin: Persönlichkeit, Gedanke, Werk," *Reformatio* [1959], pp. 261-83).

[2] One can see the growth of this sympathy by following the evolution of research on Luther in Catholicism from the beginning of this century to the present time. Cf. my work *Luther vu par les catholiques* (Neuchâtel and Paris, 1962).

[3] As Emile Doumergue correctly notes: "In relation to repugnance and hatred, one finds that Protestants rivaled Catholics" (*Le caractère de Calvin* [Paris, 1921], p. 45).

19

This calumny, which made its first appearance in 1562,[4] really dates its rise thirteen years after the death of Calvin. In 1577, a Carmelite who had been converted to evangelical ideas, Jérôme-Hermès Bolsec, after having returned to the Roman Church, published a biography of the Reformer which was no more than a vile tract. Calvin was accused in it with being ambitious, presumptuous, arrogant, cruel, evil, vindictive, and, above all, ignorant.[5] Also, he was described as an avaricious and greedy man,[6] as an imposter who claimed he could resurrect the dead, as a lover of rich fare, worst yet: as a gadabout[7] and a Sodomite, who, for his infamous habits, had been sentenced in the city of his birth, Noyon, to be branded with a red-hot iron.[8]

To complete this picture, Bolsec described the Reformer as an outcast of God, who, after having been stricken by "being eaten with lice and vermin all over his body," and after having wasted away thereby for punishment of his sins, died cursing and swearing as a blasphemer, a victim of deepest despair.[9]

It was difficult to outdo Bolsec in the area of calumny! Some forty years later, however, a vicar-general of the diocese of Rouen, Jacques Desmay, added a trait which marred the

[4] We refer to what was expressed in the two works of François Baudoin published as *Ad leges de famosis libellis et de calumniatoribus, Commentarius* and *Responsio altera ad Joan. Calvinium.* As biased as the criticism in these two works may be against the Reformer (he is accused of cowardice, of lacking heart, and of despotism), it is still mild compared to the injurious attacks of Bolsec and his followers.

[5] *L'Histoire de la vie, moeurs, actes, doctrine, constance et mort de Jean Calvin, jadis ministre de Genève.* Cf in "Archives curieuses de l'histoire de France depuis Louis XI jusqu'à Louis XVIII," edited by L. Cimber and F. Danjou, 1st ser. (Paris, 1835), V, 305.

[6] Cf. *ibid.*, pp. 325-27.

[7] Cf. *ibid.*, pp. 331-44.

[8] Cf. *ibid.*, pp. 312-13.

[9] *Ibid.*, pp. 366-67, 384.

picture of Calvin even more:[10] he pictured him as a thief.[11] In the rest of it, the Reformer appears in a slightly less unfavorable light than in Bolsec's work. He is presented to us as "the author of a religion of the table, the stomach, the fat, the flesh, the kitchen," in whom the whole reformation only tended to "establish the reign of wine, women, and song." [12]

The calumny was so gross that it was not difficult for Charles Drelincourt, pastor of a Reformed Church in Paris and one of the most popular writers of the seventeenth century among Protestants in France, to refute these slanderers of the Reformer.[13] Responding to one of the works of Richelieu,[14] who had treated Calvin terribly roughly, he did a good job of showing[15] how not only the Bolsecs and the Desmays, but also those inspired by Cardinal Richelieu[16]

[10] In his *Remarques sur la vie de Jean Calvin, tirées des registres de Noyon, ville de sa naissance* (Rouen, 1621).

[11] "And planning a long trip, in order to provide for it he stole an amount of money from his own country which had been in his protection as procurator" (*Ibid.*, in "Archives curieuses . . . ," 1st ser., V, 393).

[12] *Ibid.*, pp. 397, 398.

[13] Before Drelincourt other French theologians had defended the memory of Calvin against the calumnies of his adversaries, such as André Rivet in his *Jesuita vapulans, seu castigatio notarum Sylvestri Petrasanctae romani Loyolae sectarii, in Epistolam P. Molinaei ad Balzacum* (Leyden, 1635); and Pierre Du Moulin in his *Hyperaspistes seu defensor veritatis adversus calumnias et opprobria ingesta in veram religionem a Sylvestro Petrasancta jesuita* (Geneva, 1636).

[14] *Le Traité qui contient la méthode la plus facile et la plus assurée pour convertir ceux qui se sont séparés de l'Englise* (Paris, 1651).

[15] In his *Défense de Calvin contre l'outrage fait à sa mémoire . . .* (Geneva, 1667).

[16] Of the number of Catholic biographies of Calvin discussed by Drelincourt, it is important to mention the following: Jacques Laingey, *De vita et moribus atque rebus gestis haereticorum nostri temporis . . .* (Paris, 1581); Florimond de Raemond, *La naissance, progrès et décadence de l'hérésie de ce siècle* (Paris, 1605); Jacques Le Vasseur, *Annales de l'Eglise de Noyon, jadis dite de Vermand, ou le troisième livre des*

had perverted the truth.[17]

From then on the criticisms from the opponents of Calvin became more subtle. In his *Histoire des variations des Eglises protestantes*,[18] Bossuet inaugurated a new style of attack. Giving up the gross attacks of Bolsec and his followers and recognizing the depth of spirit, the boldness of decision, the doctrinal precision, the resolution, the seriousness, and the sincerity of the Reformer, the Bishop of Meaux formulated a series of accusations which can be summarized in three headings:[19] (1) Calvin had been very ambitious—he had been lifted up in pride "in seeing himself visible before all of Europe as on a great theatre stage," (2) An autocrat with a quick temper—he had bitten off a huge bite of the "sweet bait" of authority which always helps to make a heresiarch,[20] (3) a morose and bitter spirit, finally—he had shown a

---

antiquités, chroniques, ou plutôt histoire de la cathédrale de Noyon (Paris, 1633); and Papire Masson, *Elogia*, pt. 2 (Paris, 1638).

[17] Drelincourt did not limit himself to the apologetic purpose. He also showed in his work the place which Protestants should give to the French Reformer: "We honor the memory of Calvin as an excellent servant of God, who greatly served the advancement of His kingdom, and who was a faithful and bright light in the church. But God forbid that we should identify him as the head and the author of our religion. Our faith was preached to the world fifteen hundred years before the birth of Calvin. . . . We only receive and approve of Calvin's doctrine as it is found to conform to the Word of God contained in the Holy Scripture of the Old and the New Testaments" (*Defense de Calvin . . . ,* pp. 56-57).

[18] Published in 1688. We quote this work from the edition of Bossuet's *Oeuvres complètes* published by Gauthier frères (cf. in particular, bk. IX: *En l'an 1561. Doctrine et caractère de Calvin*, vol. XXVII, [Paris, 1828]).

[19] In the now classical volume *Bossuet, historien du protestantisme*, 3rd ed. (Paris, 1909), Alfred Rébelliau has brought together an excellent synthesis of the fundamental ideas relative to Calvin which are rather scattered in *l'Histoire des variations . . .* (cf. pp. 583-89).

[20] Bossuet, *l'Histoire des variations . . . ,* bk. IX, sec. lxxvii, p. 619.

"serious sickness" in the way he pursued his adversaries with sarcasm.[21]

This picture, which, in its unfair severity, did not lack some nuances, was terribly simplified for the nineteenth century. And so J. M. Audin, whose biography[22] was authorized for French Catholics until the end of the First World War, accused the Reformer of cowardice,[23] of an unfeeling heart,[24] of deceit,[25] of egocentrism,[26] and of despotism.[27]

"Calvin never loved," states this writer, "and no one loved him, either. One dreaded him, one feared him. No one felt drawn to him because of personal appeal. All those who knew him withdrew from him because they could not tolerate his arrogant way, his sick egoism, his vain outbursts, his un-

[21] *Ibid.*, sec. lxxxii, p. 623. Cf. sec. lxxix, pp. 620-21.

[22] *Histoire de la vie, des ouvrages et des doctrines de Calvin*, 2 vols. (Paris, 1st ed., 1841; 6th ed., 1856).

[23] Cf. *ibid.*, I, 43.

[24] Cf. *ibid.*, I, 125-26 (because Calvin on returning to Noyon, did not go to weep at his parents' tomb); I, 306-7 (because Calvin did not suffer at the death of his child); II, 335-36 (because Calvin was not affected by the decease of his wife).

[25] It is worth quoting a passage here to illustrate Audin's style: "He [Calvin] has the nature of a snake: his strength is his trickery. Until he appeared before God, he was a master of dodging. His act 'of candor' [his testament] dictated to the notary Chenelat, his dove-like whisper before Bèze—these are character traits. It must be said that he tried to fool God just as he had deceived his fellow citizens. In the history of the Reformation there is no greater actor" (*ibid.*, II, 421).

[26] Cf. *ibid.*, p. 429.

[27] Cf. *ibid.*, p. 439. In this passage Audin does not limit himself to attacking Calvin, he also takes to task those who had come to Geneva for conscience' sake; "With the pure blood of the Genevese, Calvin mixed the blood of the refugee, his praetorian guard—crooks, rascals, the bankrupt—who sat on the Consistory, who entered the Councils and became the bourgeois. And in exchange for all these honors, they brought more blemishes than the city could ever count."

measured pride." [28] For this "child of the North, . . . in-
scrutable before all eyes except God's," [29] for this man who
was so rarely emotionally moved, who was well versed in
hatred and calculating in his anger, Audin could not allow
an honorable death: he implies that the Reformer was stricken
by the hand of God and swept away with a shameful
disease.[30]

To be sure the nineteenth century produced only one
Audin! This does not mean that the non-Protestants at that
time who were interested in the biography of Calvin were
any more successful in treating their subject.[31] In spite of
his profound knowledge of the sources and the soundness of
his method, the Old Catholic scholar, F. W. Kampschulte,
professor at the University of Bonn until 1872, did not succeed in painting a satisfactory picture of the Genevan Reformer in the work which he dedicated to him.[32] For proof
one need only read the passages in which the German historian depicts the personal position of Calvin within the city
of Leman.[33] One finds there only a caricature:[34] "the discreet

[28] *Ibid.*, II, 340.

[29] *Ibid.*, I, 197.

[30] Cf. ibid., II, 415.

[31] It is not possible to review here all the works published about
Calvin in this century. One can find such a review in Adolf Zahn,
*Studien über Johannes Calvin: Die Urteile katholischer und protes-
tantischer Historiker im 19 Jahrhundert über den Reformator* (Gütersloh,
1894).

[32] *Johann Calvin: seine Kirche und sein Staat in Genf* (Leipzig:
vol. I, 1869; vol. II [published after the death of the author by
Walter Goetz], 1899).

[33] This is the subject in chap. VI, bk. VII, entitled "Calvin's
Personal Position," pp. 375-87.

[34] In his beautiful introduction to the collection of letters translated
by Rudolf Schwarz, *Johannes Calvins Lebenswerk in seinen Briefen*,
3 vols. (Neukirchen Kreis Moers, 2nd ed., 1961), Paul Wernle has
shown, following Emile Doumergue (cf. *Jean Calvin: les hommes et les*

and grave ecclesiastic from gloomy Chanoines Street" [35] appears there only as a master of forbidding appearance, who, in an atmosphere of veneration mixed with fear, exercised a domination not only over Geneva, but also beyond its city limits.

One would imagine that the twentieth century, whose merit in the eyes of posterity will certainly include the discovery of ecumenism, had been fairer to Calvin. But this is not always the case. After the effort to understand Calvin by Pierre Imbart de la Tour,[36] André Favre-Dorsaz wrote the most insidious and most destructive book about Calvin with which I am acquainted.[37] In it he contrasts Calvin with Ignatius Loyola (such a comparison is not new), and, in order to show the spiritual superiority of the founder of the Society of Jesus more clearly, he speaks of the Genevan theologian in an ironic tone, one of banter, of jest, and of contempt which is

---

choses de son temps [1899], I, 532-33 and II, 717-18), how much the Calvin of Kampschulte differs from the true Calvin. Not without reason Wernle remarks that the Bonn professor was incapable of doing justice to his hero: "When one understands only what one likes, he gives up the fine distinctions of the critical method and all genuine diligence and is not very capable of coming to a real understanding of Calvin" (I, 4). Emile G. Léonard himself, who shows no natural sympathy for the Genevan Reformer (cf. the necrological article of Alice Wemyss, in Etudes évangéliques [Aix-en-Provence, 1961], p. 159), observes that Kampschulte "is not always fair with Calvin" (cf. Bibliographie calvinienne abrégée," Calvin et la Réforme en France, 2nd ed. [Aix-en-Provence, 1959], p. 148).

[35] Cf. Kampschulte, Johann Calvin . . . , II, 387.

[36] Cf. vol. 4 of his large work on Les origines de la Réforme, entitled Calvin et l'Institution chrétienne (Paris, 1935). Some have overestimated the sympathetic aspect of the viewpoint of this French historian. We cannot agree with the judgment of Emile G. Léonard, who observes that the view of Imbart de la Tour was "perhaps too irenical and too conciliatory to give a true picture of the great heretic" ("Bibliographie calvinienne abrégée," p. 145).

[37] Calvin et Loyola: deux Réformes (Paris and Brussels, 1951).

even more distressing than the gross attacks of Bolsec. If one believes Father Favre-Dorsaz, Calvin was an acid, negative person, withdrawn, embittered and unfeeling, coldly committed pessimist;[38] an uneasy, worried, anguished man, alternately sympathetic and cruel;[39] proud,[40] a repressed sentimentalist, truly sadistic;[41] a sick man bothered by physical suffering;[42] and, finally, a dictator.[43] But this eulogism of Loyola did not limit itself to these criticisms of Calvin. It goes on to try to put in doubt Calvin's talents—talents which even his adversaries felt no need to deny. So, it says that Calvin was a superficial theologian,[44] a tendentious exegete,[45] and (the most serious accusation) a believer in whom "religious feeling" was of a rather doubtful quality:[46] he arrived at "peace of conscience" by autosuggestion; he believed in law more strongly than in the Bible; he ignored the act of suffering as much as the act of the good life; he did not know how to pray and really did not understand the spirit of Jesus Christ.[47]

[38] Cf. *ibid.*, pp. 37, 38, 47, 49, 61.
[39] Cf. *ibid.*, pp. 85, 437, 87, 90.
[40] Cf. *ibid.*, pp. 117, 122, 369.
[41] Cf. *ibid.*, pp. 193, 337.
[42] Cf. *ibid.*, pp. 362, 365.
[43] Cf. *ibid.*, pp. 236, 238, 376, 435.
[44] "He [Calvin] promised much more than he could produce. He did not possess, as strongly as he thought, the 'key to open' the Holy Scripture. . . . Doubtless it is less a question of reflecting on the authentic meaning of Scripture than of insisting long and hard and of gaining power of the reform party. . . . The *Institutes* is the theology of a very hurried layman, of an amateur lawyer, who has finally found the aim of his self-satisfaction" (*ibid.*, p. 149). This passage to which we limit ourselves gives an example of the unique style of Father Favre-Dorsaz when he speaks of Calvin.
[45] Cf. *ibid.*, p. 151.
[46] Cf. *ibid.*, p. 391.
[47] Cf. *ibid.*, pp. 193, 330, 383, 191, 392-93.

26

Introduction

Beside the picture of Calvin by Father Favre-Dorsaz, the one sketched out by Daniel-Rops[48] appears as flattery, wholly unfair though it is. For the author of *Jesus en son temps*, the Reformer is a mysterious genius, containing "something terrible and cold," a person with an exterior which was "cold and powerful,"[49] from whom emanated a kind of "Faustian influence" at the same time, "a kind of magnetic charm," "the perfect type of fanatic,"[50] a dictator who loved few if any men "in their wretchedness and weakness."[51]

If the Catholic opponents of Calvin have distorted him in this way,[52] some Protestants have caricatured him to the point that in their presentations he is not recognizable at all. Without going over the injuries done him by Jacques-Auguste and Jean-Barthélemy Galiffe,[53] who have continued their animosities toward him on and on, it is enough to quote Alfred Franklin to illustrate the unpopularity of Calvin among

---

[48] In his *Histoire de l'Eglise du Christ*, cf. the first book, *Une révolution religieuse: la Réforme protestante* (Paris, 1955), of vol. IV, *l'Eglise de la Renaissance et de la Réforme*, pp. 397-490 (chap. 6, entitled "La réussite de Jean Calvin").

[49] *Ibid.*, pp. 426, 459.

[50] *Ibid.*, p. 460.

[51] *Ibid.*, pp. 476, 446.

[52] It was not the purpose of this introduction to examine Catholic works which, unlike those we have listed, tried to understand Calvin. We only observe that *l'Histoire de l'Eglise*, ed. Augustin Fliche and Eugene Jarry, vol. 16, entitled *La crise religieuse du XVIe siécle* (Paris, 1956), contains a presentation of Calvin and Calvinism by Pierre Jourda (cf. bk. II, pp. 165-306) which shows a genuine effort at objectivity. To the picture of Calvin done by Jourda, Jean Cadier does some valuable "touching-up" in his article "La piété de Calvin," *La Revue réformée* (Saint-Germain-en-Laye, 1950), pp. 283-89.

[53] These two historians, who greatly influenced Kampschulte and his friend Cornelius, express in their works the bitterness of several old Genevese families toward Calvin, who is considered not only as a foreigner, but also as an intruder and usurper in the life of the city.

most of the nineteenth-century liberals. Franklin pictures Calvin as follows:

This great black phantom,[54] a glacial person, sombre, unfeeling, hurried, prey to an exclusive idea, who moved through the world quickly and left upon it a deep mark, irresistibly drew attention without inspiring sympathy. One resists his ascendancy, because he cannot satisfy reason and nothing in him speaks to the heart.[55]

The same author writes again of the Reformer: "Austerity without enthusiasm, an unfeeling and cold heart, never showing emotion. Did he ever laugh? Did he ever cry?" [56] The reason for all this is understandable. For Franklin, and for many other Protestants in the nineteenth century, Calvin was a sectarian[57] and a despot[58] who not only clearly stopped "the magnificent outburst which the word of Luther had started throughout Europe," but also never understood the "very essence of Christianity." [59]

[54] Under this very title, "This great black phantom . . . ," Paul de Félice refuted a number of calumnies of which Calvin had been accused. Cf. *Foi et Vie*, pp. 623-27.

[55] In the introduction, entitled "Calvin et son oeuvre," in his edition of *La Vie de J. Calvin* by Théodore de Bèze (Paris, 1869), pp. xxxix-xl.

[56] *Ibid.*, p. xxxix.

[57] Cf. *ibid.*, p. xxxvii.

[58] Cf. *ibid.*, pp. xlvi, l, lii.

[59] *Ibid.*, pp. l, lii. The hostility of Alfred Franklin is so great that he questions even the least questionable qualities of Calvin. For example, he observes that except perhaps for the *Institutes*, the Reformer's books have become "unreadable," because "in effect they all miss this high ideal which alone makes the works of the spirit lasting" (*Calvin et son oevre*, p. xli). But it is the intelligence of Calvin which Franklin tries to deny with ridiculous persistence. He writes: "He is not a thinker. He lacks the quality of eagerly seeking truth and the ideal of never ceasing to search and doubt" (p. xi). "His thought, incapable of embracing an ensemble of abstract ideas, of tracing out important lines and then determining general laws, excels in dialectics, an exercise full of details and demanding agility rather than an understanding mind" (pp.

Introduction

In spite of, or perhaps because of, the efforts of neo-Calvinism and the labors of dialectical theology trying to reevaluate the message of the sixteenth century, efforts to disparage Calvin have not stopped even today. By attacking Calvin's person, one tries to discredit his thought and that of the theologians who claim him. This twin purpose was aimed at by Oskar Pfister, a pastor and psychologist in Zürich, in a work which caused a great deal of stir.[60] In it he tried to explain the Reformer's personality only from his attitude in the sorcery affair in Peney. Because with another colleague Calvin believed it his duty to "encourage the zeal of the magistrates" [61] (in effect, he was a man of his times), he was nothing less than a sadist without love, in whom cruelty and hate were born from a morbid anguish.[62]

---

xli-xlii). "Calvin had a strong personality rather than a strong understanding" (p. 1). As is easily seen, it is not far from this accusation of lack of understanding to the accusation of ignorance suggested by Bolsec.

[60] *Calvins Eingreifen in die Hexer- und Hexenprozesse von Peney 1545 nach senier Bedeutung für Geschichte und Gegenwart: Ein kritischer Beitrag zur Charakteristik Calvins und zur gegenwärtigen Calvin-Renaissance* (Zürich, 1947).

[61] These terms are from Amédée Roget, whose impartiality is recognized by the enemies as well as the friends of Calvin, and who, in his *Histoire du peuple de Genève depuis la Réforme jusqu'à l'Escalade*, gives to the Peney events their rightful place in Calvin's ministry to Geneva (cf. vol. 2 [Geneva, 1873] pp. 178-79).

[62] Cf. Pfister, *Calvins Eingreifen* . . . , pp. 79, 97, 101. In spite of the answer which he gave to the interpretation of Fritz Büsser (*Theologische Zeitschrift* [Basel, 1948], pp. 310-13) in his article "Calvin im Lichte der Hexenprozesse von Peney," *Calvins Eingreifen* . . . pp. 411-34, Oskar Pfister seems to deserve the charges of his critic: "In his precise wording the author seems to project views which in themselves are fair and well treated, however many produce a certain impression and a subtle psychological twist. These, together with numerous similar illustrations, steer the uncritical reader into the prejudices and distortions of Pfister" (Büsser, p. 313). Cf. the important criticisms addressed to Pfister by Ernst Pfisterer in *Calvins Wirken in Genf* (Neukerchen Kreis Moers, 2nd ed., 1957), pp. 143-50.

The Humanness of John Calvin

If Pfister wronged Calvin by interpreting him only in Freudian categories, he at least saved him from a systematic disparagement. Too, his work is not the most pernicious of anti-Calvin literature. In my view the most unfair attack made on Calvin in the last several decades came from Jean Schorer. Due to the urging of this pastor of St. Peter's Cathedral in Geneva (this fact is saddening in itself), the Austrian novelist Stefan Zweig wrote a biography of Castellio[63] which (because of its unfair treatment of Calvin) has been judged by one writer as "one of the most downright pernicious falsehoods ever produced in historical literature." [64] Not content with thus having urged the publication of a wretched work, Schorer considered that it was also necessary to defend it, after the death of its author, against the solid criticisms which had been raised against it. So he published a work, composed in large part of multilated and falsified quotations, with the purpose of accrediting the legend of a dictator—Calvin.[65]

This is enough to illustrate the fact that the Reformer of Geneva has not received any better treatment from Protestant hands than from his Catholic opponents. It is enough also to show that in the opinion of both, Calvin is a kind of monster whose memory is enough to result in absolute recoil and rejection. But was he really that kind of man—this

---

[63] *Castellio gegen Calvin, oder ein Gewissen gegen die Gewalt* (Vienna, 1936). Translated into French by Alzir Hella as *Castellion contre Calvin, ou conscience contre violence* (Paris, 1946).

[64] Roland de Pury in his survey of Zweig's work in *Réforme*, April 12, 1947.

[65] Jean Schorer, *Jean Calvin et sa dictature d'après des historiens anciens et modernes* (Geneva, 1948). In their work *Calvin, Stefan Zweig et M. Jean Schorer* (Geneva, 1949), Henri Delarue and Paul-F. Geisendorf pointed out in an irrefutable way the lack of intellectual integrity of the one who was then pastor of St. Peter's Cathedral (cf. pp. 21 ff., 53 ff.).

man who died four hundred years ago, May 27, 1564? Was he really "antihuman," [66] or inhuman, as they would lead us into believing? And their grievances, all the accusations which have been mentioned, can be summarized in these two descriptive terms. Of course the answer is "no," and in order to prove it we will not try to refute them successively. Such a job would be possible but not practical. In a more practical way we propose, by using his correspondence, mainly to show the true John Calvin, who was husband and father, friend and pastor. In this way we hope to set forth his real humanness.[67]

[66] We use this adjective as we recall the judgment of Orentin Douen, who in contrasting Marot and Calvin stated in relation to the latter: "Calvin is the kind of dogmatic authoritarian, anti-liberal, anti-artistic, anti-human and anti-Christian, the opposite of the gentle and virile spirit of Jesus, who fought against all forms of religion exterior to the soul, and addressed himself directly to the conscience, in order thereby to nourish moral sensitivity and feeling" (*Clément Marot et le psautier huguenot* [Paris, 1878], I, 387). It is certainly Calvin's theology which was aimed at through his personality.

[67] Peter Vogelsanger, who correctly observed in "Johannes Calvin: Persönlichkeit, Gedanke, Werk" that behind the criticisms directed against Calvin is hidden an opposition to the Reformation (p. 262), writes in agreement: "The more one becomes acquainted with the real Calvin, the stronger becomes one's respect for him, and not only because of his great talents, but also because of his humanness" (p. 267). The article by Father François Biot, O.P., "Humanité de Jean Calvin," in *Découverte de l'oecuménisme* (Paris, 1961), pp. 368-75, which shows a genuine sympathy toward Calvin, will not add anything significant to this subject. On the other hand, one would find helpful pointers in the work of Fritz Büsser, *Calvins Urteil über sich selbst* (Zürich, 1950). Cf. my article "Les discours à la première personne dans les sermons de Calvin," to appear in *Revue d'histoire et de philosophie religieuses.* Now available in *Regards contemporaines sur Jean Calvin* . . . (Paris, 1965), pp. 206-38.

Chapter 1
Husband and Father[1]

Responding in his *Traité des scandales* to Catholic objections according to which the Reformation occurred with its main object being the desire of certain priests to be married, Calvin could say in all sincerity: "After God delivered me from it [that is, the Roman Church], I waited a long time before taking a wife." [2] Actually it was at the age of thirty-one that

[1] On this subject cf. Jules Bonnet, *Récits du XVIᵉ siècle*, (2nd ed. Paris, 1875), I, 75-101; August Lang, "Das häusliche Leben Johannes Calvins," an article which appeared in June, 1893, in the supplement of the *Allgemeine Zeitung* in Munich and was reprinted in *Reformation und Gegenwart* (Detmold, 1918), pp. 39–71; Emile Doumergue, *Jean Calvin: les hommes et les choses de son temps* (Lausanne, 1902), II, 441-78; Jean Palès, "Calvin intime: son mariage, son foyer" in *Foi et Vie* (1909), pp. 627-33; Anna Katterfeld, *Idelette, die Gattin Calvins* (Basel and Leipzig, 1939); and T. H. L. Parker, *Portrait of Calvin* (London, 1954), pp. 63-77.

[2] *Opuscules*, p. 1208, and *Trois traités* (Paris and Geneva, 1934), p. 275.

the Reformer became married.[3] Not that as a young man he was opposed to marriage in principle! On more than one occasion he raised his voice against ecclesiastical celibacy. He wrote to an unidentified person, a pastor with whom he had doubtless discussed the question of the legitimacy of marriage:[4] "I am inclined to be hostile to the celibate even though I am not married and don't know if I ever will be. If I should take a wife, it would be in order to dedicate myself more completely to the Lord, being greatly freed from many worries." [5]

These words tell us that the reformers had been involved in a kind of adventure of which it is very difficult for us moderns to conceive. Bound to the service of the Word of God, they had risked their very lives for their faith. Therefore, it is not surprising at all if the young humanist who had been exiled from France following the incident of the placards opposing the mass, if the author pressed to write the *Institutes of the Christian Religion,* if the organizer in charge of the Genevan Church, if the pastor who was forced out of his first parish did not even dream of getting married. When one fights in the front lines, he does not even consider sharing all the dangers which he faces with a wife!

It was in Strasbourg, where he had settled in September, 1538, and where besides assuming duties as pastor to French refugees he was also professor of exegesis, that the Reformer

[3] Approximately August 10, 1539, as calculated by August Lang (cf. "Das häusliche Leben J. C.," p. 49). Farel, who was at this time in Strasbourg, probably performed the wedding ceremony.

[4] I do not know the basis of Jules Bonnet's identification of this correspondent with Ambroise Blaurer, pastor in Tübingen (cf. *Récit du XVI*e *siècle,* p. 79). Nor do I know why Jean Palès dates this document in 1536 (cf. "Calvin intime," p. 628). Entitled "Caelibatum in ministro non ita requirendum esse," it appears in *Consilia,* published by Baum, Cunitz, and Reuss (cf. O.C., X/1, 226-29).

[5] O.C., X/1, 228.

faced the question of his own marriage. We know that in the course of the Frankfort Conference of 1539, at which representatives of the two confessions had gathered for discussion, during a meal Melanchthon made fun of Calvin, who had been rather pensive, by saying that "he was dreaming of getting married." [6] This pleasantry was perhaps not without basis. If one remembers the bonds of friendship which developed between Melanchthon and Calvin, it is not impossible to see in this story an illustration of the confidence which the pastor of the French church in Strasbourg had in the Wittenberg theologian.

Scarcely had he returned from Frankfort than Calvin needed money very badly. Since he had not received a salary for six months, he was forced to sell some of his books in order to exist.[7] However, this situation could not last forever. He received with gratitude the decision of the authorities of

[6] The story is told by Antoine de la Fontaine in a letter to Calvin, January 13, 1541, sending his best wishes concerning Calvin's wedding. Cf. O.C., XI, 143-44, and Herminjard, VII, 6.

[7] Cf., for example, his letters to Farel in March and April, 1539. In the first he writes: "The Waldensian brothers owe me a crown. I had loaned one to them and had given another to a messenger who came with my brother. . . . I have asked them to return it to you. If they do it, please keep it since I owe so much to you. I will pay the rest when I can. At the present I am in a bind and cannot pay a cent. It is amazing to see how many extra expenses I have, and besides it is necessary that I live on what I have if I do not want to be dependent on the brothers" (O.C., X/2, 332, and Herminjard, V, 270). In the second of these letters, after having expressed his appreciation of Farel's generosity and of his friends' loans, which aided him so much, Calvin adds: "I have decided not to appeal to your kindness again nor to theirs, unless forced by a terribly great need. Windelin [that is, Rihel], the printer to whom I have given the rights to my little book [that is, the 2nd Latin edition of the *Institutes*], will give me what I need for extra expenses. With my books which are still in Geneva there will be enough to pay my landlord until next winter. For the future the Lord will provide" (O.C., X/2, 340, and Herminjard, V, 291).

Strasbourg to grant him a florin a week (the salary of a suffragan) beginning May 1, 1539. Did the prospect of receiving this modest (not to say ridiculous) sum cause him to think of starting a home? [8] We don't really know. But one fact is sure: on May 19, 1539, Calvin revealed in a letter to his friend Farel that he was looking for a wife. "Remember well what I am looking for in her. I am not of that crazy breed of lovers, who, stricken by the beauty of a woman, love even her faults. The only beauty which captivates me is that of a chaste, kind, modest, thrifty, patient woman, who I might finally hope would be attentive to my health." [9]

The young girl about whom Farel had talked with Calvin doubtless did not comply with this description. Unless one assume with Jules Bonnet that "the ardent missionary who displayed so much marvelous eloquence among the rough folk of the Jura and the Alps was more skillful in handling the thunderbolts of God's Word than in taking care of delicate matters." [10] As a matter of fact, nine months later Calvin was still not married. On February 6, 1540, he wrote to a pastor in Neuchâtel in order to confide the embarrassing situation in which he found himself. He states:

[8] I cannot accept all the influencing motives which Anna Katterfeld ascribes to Calvin's marriage. If no text allows us to say with her that the Reformer was moved to jealousy by the happy marriage of Viret (cf. *Idelette*, p. 6), it is equally erroneous to speak, as T. H. L. Parker likewise did (cf. *Portrait of Calvin*, p. 69), of the beautiful example of married life given Calvin by Farel (cf. *Idelette*, p. 7) . . . who remained celibate for sixty-nine years. As to the feeling of loneliness and the desire to have children (*Idelette*, pp. 6-8) that Anna Katterfeld attributes to the Reformer, these belong in the area of romantic imagination. On the other hand, Doumergue's argument offers more probability according to which Calvin would have been "certainly urged by Bucer, the great apostle of marriage" (*Jean Calvin*, p. 448).

[9] O.C., X/2, 348, and Herminjard, V, 314.

[10] *Récits du XVIᵉ siècle*, pp. 80-81.

The Humanness of John Calvin

I have been offered a young girl. She is from a noble family and the dowry exceeds my present needs. I turn away from this marriage for two reasons: she does not speak our language and I fear that she may bear her lineage and her education too much in mind. Her brother, a man of deep piety, is insisting and with no other motive except, blinded by his love for me, he is neglecting his own interests. Animated with the same kind of enthusiasm, his wife fights alongside him in such a way that I would almost have been reduced to declaring myself conquered if the Lord had not delivered me.[11]

Evidently the situation was terribly embarrassing. Calvin, who had legitimate reasons for not desiring this marriage, but who through a refusal feared offending a family motivated in his view by the best intentions, believed that he might get out of the situation by requiring one condition: he requested that the young noble lady promise to learn French. Since she would want some time to make her decision, he would profitably use this delay in order to try to become engaged to someone else.[12] Without further delay he would request his brother to go and ask for the hand of another person. "If she answers to her reputation," he wrote Farel, "she would bring, if not any money, a good enough dowry. Actually she is complimented by those who know her in a most flattering way." And Calvin added, he would then set his heart upon

[11] O.C., XI, 12 and Herminjard, VI, 167 .

[12] It would have been easy for Calvin, and more in conformity with the hard and cold character which has been attributed to him so often, to reject the advances of the relatives of the young girl uncategorically and bring the matter to an end. As unpleasant as the action of the Reformer might appear to us in this matter (it is not without cause that Anna Katterfeld tries to idealize [Cf. *Idelette*, p. 14]), we are shown a man desirous, though clumsy and awkward, of not hurting those who like him so much.

marriage: "If, as I strongly hope, she accepts my offer, the wedding will not be delayed beyond next March 10." [13]

Three weeks later Calvin believed this matter to be sufficiently advanced to write Farel:

We are waiting on the young lady until a little after Easter, but if you promise to come for sure, we will postpone the wedding until your arrival. We will have plenty of time to set the date. Therefore I first request of you, as an important favor, that you come, and then that you confirm your coming. In any case, it is necessary that someone come to perform the ceremony. And so far as I am concerned, I would rather have you than anyone else.[14]

The pastor of the French church in Strasbourg had been too optimistic about an early wedding. This is apparent in a letter of March 29, 1540, sent to his colleague in Neuchâtel. The virtuous yet poor young lady of whom he was thinking had not yet responded to his request. The family of the rich aristocratic lady had taken advantage of this delay by returning to the attack. Pressed to wed the young noble lady, Calvin wrote to Farel: "I would never do it, unless the Lord entirely deprived me of reason. However, because it is difficult to refuse, above all, those who overwhelm me with their kindness, I deeply desire to be freed from this difficulty. I hope that it will be soon." [15] By the middle of May the situation

[13] O.C., XI, 12 and Herminjard, VI, 168.
[14] Letter of February 26, 1540, O.C., XI, 25 and Herminjard, VI, 191-92. Emile Doumergue (cf. *Jean Calvin*, p. 449) and Anna Katterfeld (cf. *Idelette*, p. 14) are in error to connect this passage with the following words: "Oh! If only I could explain to you how I feel, and, in turn, hear your advice." These words immediately precede the quotation in the above text. It was not to his matrimonial plans that he referred but to the theological problems posed by the Caroli affair.
[15] O.C., XI, 30, and Herminjard, VI, 199-200.

had not changed.[16] Finally, on June 21, 1540, Calvin informed Farel, several days after the end of his engagement with the one who brought only a good reputation as her dowry, he had had to break off because of some rumors which had been reported to him concerning her. And, confessing his misfortune, he stated: "I fear that if you want to attend my wedding, you may not come until much later. I have not yet found a wife, and I am asking myself whether I should search any more.[17]

In view of these tentative matrimonial plans, one is justified in being rather surprised. If Calvin wanted to be married, why did he allow his friends the task of finding the one who would correspond to the feminine ideal which he had set forth? In order to understand such an attitude we must remind ourselves that at this time not one of the protagonists of the Reformation had a romantic idea of love. Even the marriage of Luther—and we are well aware of the tenderness which the Wittenberg Reformer had for Katherine von Bora— seems to be, in the beginning, dictated by motives which had nothing to do with feeling.[18] Therefore, one may speak of an "arranged marriage," if one wishes, but without forgetting that the matrimonial steps of the sixteenth century did not exclude happiness *a priori* between those joined, who, God bless them, were of the same mind.

It was a marriage of this type in which Calvin was involved. Less than two months after sending the letter, in which, in

[16] Cf. the letter to Farel which Herminjard dates *circa* May 13, 1540, and in which Calvin states: "My affairs are at the same place as before" (O.C., XI, 39 and Herminjard, VI, 221).

[17] O.C., XI, 52 and Herminjard, VI, 238.

[18] August Lang correctly states: "However, one must keep in mind that the marriage contract at that time was generally very businesslike in character and this stood in the foreground. . . . There are no sentimental love stories from those days." (P. 47.)

a way, something was said condemning the celibate life,
Christophe Fabri, pastor in Thonon, sent Calvin greetings to
his wife.[19] At the same time, Farel wrote Fabri telling him
about the marriage of Calvin with an "upright and honest"
and "even pretty" woman.[20] On Bucer's advice, the pastor
of the French church in Strasbourg had married about August
10, 1540.[21] He married Idelette de Bure, the widow of an
Anabaptist citizen of Liège[22] who had returned to the Reformed faith shortly before his death. She brought him no
wealth except two children born during her first marriage,
a boy whose name remains unknown to us[23] and a girl,
Judith, whom the Reformer looked after as a father.

The task facing the newlyweds was not an easy one. A
little after getting settled in Strasbourg, Calvin had received
his friend Antoine into his home, as well as a number of
boarders: some young Frenchmen who were students in Strasbourg and a noble woman along with her son and a servant.
It was necessary, in order to live smoothly in this small and

---

[19] Cf. letter of August 17, 1540, O.C., XI, 77, and Herminjard,
VI, 275.

[20] Letter of August 28, 1540, O.C., XI, 78, and Herminjard, VI,
285.

[21] It is to Nicolas Colladon, colleague and biographer of Calvin,
that we owe this information. Colladon summarizes in one sentence the
life of Idelette de Bure with Calvin: "There was among this number
[that is, among the Anabaptists converted by Calvin] one named Jean
Stordeur, a native of Liège, who had died of the plague in Strasbourg.
Some time later Calvin married his widow, named Odilette or Idelette
de Bure, a serious and upright woman (he did this as a result of the
advice of Bucer), and with her lived happily even though our Lord
did not give them children, for though she had a son by him, the
baby died very soon" [O.C., XXI, 62]).

[22] And not French, as T. H. L. Parker states (cf. *Portrait of Calvin*,
p. 70).

[23] Parker is mistaken in naming him Jacques (cf. *ibid.*). This was the
name of the child Calvin had by Idelette de Bure.

diverse "world," to work out the tensions between the terribly sensitive Antoine and the aristocratic Madame du Verger, who so readily spoke hurtful words. The Reformer worked at it very hard, even at the expense of his health, because tensions at home affected him deeply. In spite of these difficulties the newlyweds were happy. We know this indirectly by means of an account which Calvin gave, in a letter to Farel, of a sickness which attacked him and his wife some six weeks after the wedding. As if reproaching himself for such deep joy in his new life, since others were perhaps at the same time being persecuted for their faith, he wrote: "Truly, lest our marriage be too happy, the Lord has from the first moderated our joy so that it might not run beyond itself." [24]

But a more formidable test was going to try the new home. At the end of February, 1541, Calvin was appointed by the authorities in Strasbourg as a delegate to the Ratisbon Colloquy. It started without him, but Melanchthon requested his participation because he had "a very fine reputation among learned men." [25] Hardly had he arrived than he learned that the plague had hit Strasbourg in all its fury. His household had not been spared. Two of his favorite boarders, the deacon of his church, Claude Féray, a worthy young Greek student who was headed for the ministry, and Louis de Richebourg, a young Norman noble, had been swept away by the terrible sickness. His friend Antoine had fled to a neighboring village to escape the plague. And his wife had taken refuge with a relative who lived nearby.

In the midst of such disaster, Calvin could not hide his suffering. He was not stoical or impassive as he has so often been pictured. He wrote Farel:

[24] Not dated, this letter is probably from the end of September, 1540. O.C., XI, 83 and Herminjard, VI, 312.

[25] O.C., V, lvi and Emile Doumergue, *Jean Calvin* . . . , II, 626.

Husband and Father

To the cruelty of the sorrow has been violently added an anxious fear for those who survive. Night and day my wife is in my thoughts, deprived of advice since she is denied her husband's presence. Bereavement over my excellent Charles [that is, de Richebourg] torments me in a particular way—he, who in four days had been deprived of his only brother and of his teacher whom he loved as a father. These events bring me such sadness that they completely overwhelm my soul and break my spirit.[26]

And a few days later, in a message to Pierre Viret, a reformer in the canton of Vaud, Calvin cried out as he thought of Idelette and the guests in his home who still lived: 'What makes my grief grow even more is that I hear it said that they are in danger and there is no way that I can help them, or, at the least, comfort them a little by my presence." [27]

Returning to Strasbourg at the end of June, 1541,[28] Calvin was joyful to find his wife safe and sound. A bit later they settled in Geneva where the authorities had invited him. Henceforth it was in this city that their lives unfolded. It is very difficult to trace their married life together too precisely.[29] Actually, the information relative to this subject is rare because Calvin always practiced remarkable discretion in relation to his personal affairs.[30] However, one pointer is given to us which is beautiful, because it allows us to see Idelette de Bure not as a retiring companion, but as a true

[26] Letter of March 29, 1541, O.C., XI, 175 and Herminjard, VII, 55-56.

[27] Letter of April 2, 1541, O.C., XI, 181 and Herminjard, VII, 65.

[28] Cf. Herminjard, VII, 157, n. 2.

[29] Jules Bonnet gives a description based more on romantic history than on actual history (cf. pp. 89-99).

[30] August Lang has correctly observed about the nature of this reserve that it came from the objectivity of the French Reformer, who, in contrast to the subjectivity of Luther, approximated "old-fashioned temperament" (cf. "Das häusliche Leben J.C.," p. 41).

collaborator with her husband. Even though she was pregnant at the time, she went to the bedside of the Syndic Ami Porral, who was at the point of death. Calvin told Viret: "She urged him to be of good courage whatever might happen and to believe that she had not come by accident, but that she had been sent by the wonderful wisdom of God in order also to serve the gospel." [31]

Several weeks after having thus shared the consolation of the Christian faith with a dying person, Idelette brought a son into the world. The very day of the birth (July 28, 1542), Calvin expressed his fears to Farel: "Since my wife is in labor and not without danger, my thoughts are elsewhere." [32] And in a letter to Viret, doubtless a little later, he repeated: "My brother, I will tell you what great fears I have as I write. My wife is going to give birth but not without grave danger, because her pregnancy is not yet full-term. May God protect us!" [33] The child, named Jacques,[34] did not live. One can imagine how deeply this grief affected the parents. Calvin lets us see some of this sadness as he writes to Viret: "Certainly the Lord has afflicted us with a deep and painful wound in the death of our beloved son. But he is our Father: he knows what is best for his children." [35] To these moving words, in which grief is alleviated by faith, he echoes the answer which the Reformer (just before his death) would address to François Baudoin, who reproached him by saying that the fact that he had left no descendants was a divine

[31] Letter of June 16, 1542, O.C., XI, 409 and Herminjard, VIII, 56.

[32] O.C., XI, 418, and Herminjard, VIII, 81.

[33] O.C., XI, p. 420, and Herminjard, VIII, pp. 82-83.

[34] Cf. letter to Farel of August 21, 1547, O.C., XII, 580-81.

[35] Letter of August 19, 1542, O.C., XI, 430, and Herminjard, VIII, 109.

curse:[36] "The Lord gave me a little son and then he took him away." And Calvin added, to refute the allegation that he had never experienced fatherhood: "I reply that in Christendom I have ten thousand children." [37]

Idelette had difficulty in recovering from her hard pregnancy and childbirth. In 1545, at the time when Calvin was taking some steps to recover his stepson, who for some unknown reason was separated from them,[38] she became gravely ill. One can follow the development of her condition through her husband's letters, from the time "she was put to bed" until the time when she appeared to be a "resurrected wife." [39] Actually, this resurrection was only a remission. Idelette never recovered her health. After having hoped for her recovery,[40] Calvin began to dread the worst. He wrote in this vein to Viret: "I fear something contrary to my hopes. . . . May

[36] Against Jules Bonnet, who believes (cf. *Récits du XVIᵉ siècle*, I, 93), and August Lang, who is inclined to believe (cf. "Das häusliche Leben J.C.," p. 57) that Calvin had two other children who died at an early age, Emile Doumergue shows beyond the shadow of a doubt that the Reformer had only one child (cf. *Jean Calvin . . .*, pp. 471-72). The argument of the Dean of Montauban is ignored by Anna Katterfeld (cf. *Idelette . . .*, p. 47), who follows the mistake of Bonnet and Lang.

[37] *Réponse de M. Jean Calvin aux injures de Balduin* (1562), in *Opuscules*, p. 1987.

[38] This whole question is still very obscure. As the editors of the *Opera Calvini* remarked (cf. XII, 153, n. 2), it is worthy of the insight of an Oedipus. What is certain is that the son whom Idelette de Bure had during her first marriage was an object of the interest and the preoccupations of Calvin. Cf. letters to Hubert, August 31, 1545, and January 21, 1546, in O.C., XII, 153-54 and 261-62.

[39] That is, from September to October, 1545. Cf. letters to M. and Madame de Falais (O.C., XII, 169-72 and 173-74, and Bonnet, I, 129-32 and pp. 133-34), to Farel (O.C. XII, 189-90), to Viret (O.C., XII, 200-201, and Bonnet, I, 137-38).

[40] Cf. letter to Christophe Fabri, written before March, 1546, in which Calvin said in relation to his wife: "However, I hope that she will recover and will regain her strength little by little" (O.C., XII, 241).

God show favor toward us." [41] During the following summer (1548) there was a slight improvement. She improved enough to go to Lausanne: she hoped to be helpful in Viret's home where a baby was expected. In spite of her devotion, she could not be very helpful. Calvin excused her for this as he wrote: "My wife would have been a great help to you; I am terribly regretful. As I can guess, she has not been of much help to the new mother. Because of her health, she herself needs to be constantly helped by others." [42] From then on, and in spite of a last reprieve which led Calvin to say (though aware of the gravity of the sickness): "The Lord still does more than we could hope," [43] the events were inexorably going to follow their course.[44] Idelette died on March 29, 1549.[45] Her husband helped her to the end. After assuring her that he would be an attentive father to the children whom she had had during her first marriage, he spoke to her about the grace of Christ, the transitoriness of this life, and the hope of eternal life. Then, stricken with sorrow, he stepped aside to pray before seeing her die peacefully.

The loss of his wife was a terrible blow to Calvin. In two letters, addressed to Farel and Viret, he recounted the edifying death of this one who, according to his letters, had occupied a discreet but very real place.[46] His account of the death is deeply moving. In spite of his desire not to speak at

[41] Cf. letter of December 23, 1547, O.C., XII, 638.

[42] Letter probably dating from June, 1548, O.C., XII, 732.

[43] Letter to Viret, January 21, 1549, O.C., XIII, 163.

[44] Cf. letter to Viret, March 10, 1549, in which Idelette is said to be back in bed, O.C., XIII, 215.

[45] Cf. O.C., XIII, 226, n. 1.

[46] One example: Calvin never sent letters to his friends the Falais without also sending them greetings from his wife. So, from 1545 to 1549, Idelette is mentioned no less than thirty times in the French correspondence.

all of himself,[47] he could not stop himself from expressing his feelings: "I am trying as much as possible not to be completely overwhelmed by grief," he wrote to Farel.

Besides, my friends surround me and do not fail to bring some comfort to my soul's sadness. . . . I consume my grief in such a way that I have not interrupted my work. . . . Farewell, brother and faithful friend. . . . May the Lord Jesus strengthen your spirit and mine in this great sadness, which would have broken me had He not extended his hand from on high; He whose service includes the relief of the broken, the strengthening of the weak, the renewal of those who are tired.[48]

And to Viret, Calvin says:

Though the death of my wife has been a very cruel thing for me, I try as much as possible to moderate my grief. And my friends fulfill their duty in a fine way. But I confess that for them and for me, the results are less than might be hoped for. However, the few results that I obtain help very little. Actually, you know the tenderness or rather the softness of my soul. . . . Of course, the reason for my sorrow is not an ordinary one. I am deprived of my excellent life companion, who, if misfortune had come, would have been my willing companion not only in exile and sorrow, but even in death.[49]

Calvin never forgot Idelette. Three months after her death, he wrote to Bucer: "I survived my better half, for recently the

[47] August Lang neatly characterizes the tone of these two letters of Calvin as he writes: "Here he also remained true to his style of objective narrative. But it is a narrative under whose rather quiet appearance we are able to see much better the decided lament, mixed with pain and love and at the same time with awe as he ponders the question of death" ("Das häusliche Leben J.C.," p. 61).

[48] Letter of April 2, 1549, O.C., XIII, 228, 229.

[49] Letter of April 7, 1549, O.C., XIII, 230.

Lord called my wife to him." [50] Less than a year later he dedicated to the doctor who had devotedly attended her, Benoît Textor, his *Commentary on II Thessalonians*.[51] And when his colleague in the French church in Frankfort was widowed, he wrote him a letter of consolation which began as follows: "What a cruel wound, what grief the death of your wonderful wife must give you. I know from my own experience. I recall how difficult it was for me seven years ago to recover from the same kind of grief." [52] To these words, which show just how much the death of Idelette had affected him, he added the words of consolation which doubtless had strengthened him. He reminded the grieving husband that he would rediscover the woman he loved on the day when he would leave this world.

Such a man was the Reformer: a man capable of affection and tenderness, who, without indulging in disordered raptures, suffered deeply as a result of the death of his wife and his son. It is a great distance from this tender and sensitive being to the cold monster invented by legend. The husband of Idelette de Bure and the father of Jacques Calvin had nothing in common with the bloodless phantom whose image was spread about by malicious slander.

[50] Letter of June 28, 1549, *O.C.*, XX, 394.

[51] Cf. *Comm. N. T.*, IV, 151. In his dedication, the Reformer specifically says: "The memory and recollection which I so clearly have of my wife reminds me every day of how much I owe you: not only because many times you may have helped us by your aid and relief, as on one occasion when she was cured of a terrible and dangerous sickness and restored to health, but also because even in the last illness which came to us, you labored very hard and did everything that was possible to help her."

[52] Cf. letter to Richard Vauville (the date is uncertain), *O.C.*, XV, 867.

Chapter 2
Friend[1]

As Emile Doumergue has correctly pointed out, "no other reformer had the personal attraction which Calvin had."[2] Without exaggerating, one may even say that there were few men who developed as many friendships as he and who knew how to retain not only the admiration, but also the personal

[1] On this subject, cf. Jules Bonnet, "Les amitiés de Calvin: Joachim Vadian-Martin Bucer," in BSHPF (1869), pp. 257-68; *Récits du XVI*^e *siècle*, I, 102-42 (Charles de Jonvillers), I, 143-75 (Guillaume Farel, Pierre Viret, and Théodore de Bèze), II, 1-38 (Laurent de Normandie); *Nouveaux récits du XVI*^e *siècle* (Paris, 1870), pp. 1-26 (Mathurin Cordier) and pp. 171-209 (the marquis de Vico); *Derniers récits du XVI*^e *siècle* (Paris, 1876), pp. 1-24 (Philip Melanchthon); Emile Doumergue, *Jean Calvin* . . . , I, 66-68, 75-77, 132-40, 181-85; II, 376-89, 545-61; III, 527-645 *passim*; and VII (Neuilly-sur-Seine, 1927), 432-42; Rudolf Schwarz, "Calvins Freundschaft," in *Reformierte Kirchen-Zeitung* (Nuremberg, 1909), pp. 91-93, 97-100, 106-7, 114-15, 123-25, 130-33; Leopold Monod, *Le caractère de Calvin d'après ses lettres* (Lyon, 1912), pp. 9-17; Henri Meylan, "Une amitié au XVIe siècle: Farel, Viret, Calvin" in *Silhouettes du XVI*^e *siècle*, (Lausanne, 1943), pp. 27-50; and Fritz Büsser, *Calvins Urteil über sich selbst* (Zürich, 1950), pp. 75-80.

[2] *Le caractère de Calvin*, p. 41.

affection of these friends.[3] This fact is often ignored and now deserves to be pointed out.

At every stage of his life, from adolescence to old age, the Reformer strengthened close personal relationships, which, except for a few rare exceptions,[4] resisted the trials of life and the wear of time.

From the time he was a small schoolboy in the Capettes School in the village of his birth, Noyon, Calvin developed a friendship with the sons of Louis de Hangest, Lord of Montmor.[5] When they left for Paris in order to study there Calvin accompanied them. This was in 1523. Twenty years later, after life had separated the commoner's son from his

---

[3] Paul Wernle has correctly stated: "The subject of Calvin as friend must be a most important part of any biography of his life. He had a distinguished association which was marked by candor, openness, but also tact with these men [that is, Melanchthon, Bullinger, Farel, and Bucer]!" ("Geleitwort," in Rudolf Schwarz, *Johannes Calvins Lebenswerk in seinen Briefen*, I, 12).

[4] Of all the friendships which Calvin developed, only three did not last: those with Louis Du Tillet, Jacques de Falais, and François Baudoin. The Reformer broke his relations with Du Tillet after he had renounced the Reformed faith and returned to the Catholic church (cf. letter of October 20, 1538, O.C., X/2, 269-72, Herminjard, V, 161-65, and Bonnet, I, 19-24). Jacques de Falais alienated himself from the Reformer by openly opposing him in his disagreement with Jerome Bolsec (cf. letter not dated but doubtless from 1552, in O.C., XIV, 448-50, and Bonnet, I, 363-66), As to François Baudoin, who, according to Bayle, changed his faith "at least seven times," Calvin was very indulgent with him for a long time before condemning his perfidy in 1561 in a tract entitled *Résponse à un certain moyenneur rusé, qui, sous couleur de pacification, a tâché de rompre le droit cours de l'Evangile au Royaume de France* (cf. *Opuscules*, pp. 1885-1918). Not content to have given proof of his change in the area of faith, Baudoin had advised the King of Navarre and the Cardinal of Lorraine to oppose the Reformed theologians before some representatives of Lutheranism expressly sent for from Germany.

[5] On the relation between the Hangest and the Calvin families, cf. Abel Lefranc, *La Jeunesse de Calvin* (Paris, 1888), pp. 7, 13-14, 133-34.

noble friends, the friendship which had begun during their youth remained vibrant. The youngest son of the noble family, whose given name is unknown, wrote to the Reformer to tell him of his plans to settle in Geneva. Like many citizens of Noyon, he had been won over by the Reformation. Calvin was ready and eager to receive him. Better than that, since his old friend from the noble class was still single, Calvin dreamed of arranging a marriage. Since he was "a young man . . . of good disposition, very human and easy to get along with," Calvin himself would be willing to set things in motion for him to find a wife of his station in life.[6]

Very different from the friendship with Montmor, but no less secure, is that which Calvin developed during his earliest years of study in Paris with Maturin Cordier, regent at the Collège de la Marche.[7] This most remarkable teacher of his time was more than thirty years older than his pupil. One might expect an insuperable generation gap between them. This was not the case. Calvin retained a high regard for the man who had taught him Latin. To this appreciation was added a feeling of solidarity created by a common faith because Cordier adopted Reformed ideas.[8] Also, when in 1536 Calvin needed a principal for the school in Geneva, he immediately invited Cordier to come from Bordeaux.[9] The two men had the same kind of friendship in Geneva. And both

[6] Cf. letter to M. de Falais, September 10, 1547, O.C., XII, 586-87 and Bonnet, I, 224-25. In his letter of September 29, 1547, to the same person, Calvin makes mention of the delay of M. de Montmor, who had been detained in Noyon following some iconoclastic troubles (Cf. O.C., XII, 594 and Bonnet, I, 226-27).

[7] Cf. the beautiful work of Jules Le Coultre, *Maturin Cordier et les origines de la pédagogie protestante dans les pays de langue française* (Neuchâtel, 1926).

[8] Cf. *ibid.*, p. 37.

[9] Cf. *ibid.*, p. 124.

of them were banished from Geneva for not being willing to accept the "Bernese traditions" which the civil power wanted to impose on the church. Though they were separated again by circumstances, their friendship was not destroyed nor changed. In 1550 Calvin dedicated his *Commentary on I Thessalonians* to his former teacher who was then principal of the Collège du Lausanne.

Calvin stated:

In truth you play an important role in my present work. Under your direction I first began my serious studies, and now at least I have progressed to a point of being able in some way to benefit the church of God. At the time my father sent me as a young boy to Paris, I had only a small knowledge of Latin. God willed that I should meet you as my teacher very soon so that you might truly set me on the right road and in the correct way of learning so that as a result I could later have benefited no better . . . although circumstances did not allow me to enjoy your instruction for very long. However, the instruction and skill which you were able to give me served me well later. It is only proper for me to confess and acknowledge being indebted to you deeply for whatever progress I have made since then. Of this truth I sincerely want to give a testimony to those who will come after us, so that, if they receive any help from my writings, they will know that in part it has come from you.[10]

One could relate other examples to illustrate the lasting friendships developed by Calvin during his first residence in Paris.[11] They would only confirm the judgment of the great scholar Abel Lefranc, who said:

[10] *Comm. N. T.*, IV, 109.

[11] It is important to speak in particular of his relationships with Pierre Robert, surnamed Olivetan, the translator of the Bible in 1535, and with the sons of the king's physician; Nicholas Cop, who in his capacity as rector of the University of Paris delivered the famous speech

Friend

If one is trying . . . to determine the character, the habits, and the propensities of the future Reformer during this period, one can easily find evidence that he was not a morose and somber person, a lonely and rather bilious student, as he has been sometimes described. The friendships which he inspired in the circles in which he lived at this time, among his teachers as well as among his colleagues, are strong enough testimonies to the fact that he knew how to combine with his serious and intense commitment to work, an affability and graciousness which won everyone over to him.[12]

The sociability of Calvin is not contradicted during his time at the universities of Orléans and Bourges, where, due to his father's wishes, he pursued studies in law. Among the friendships dating from this period,[13] the most moving is undoubtedly the one which bound the future Reformer to the jurist François Daniel. The correspondence which they maintained between 1530 and 1536 [14] and by means of which

---

of November 1, 1533; and also Michel Cop, who followed the Reformer to Geneva and became a pastor there.

[12] *La jeunesse de Calvin* (Paris, 1888), p. 70. Cf. Lucien Febvre: "Before the classical pictures of Calvin . . . there had lived in this world a little Picard—lively, alert, with bright and sparkling eyes—a very fascinating Picard with qualities of frankness, openness, thoughtfulness" ("Une mise en place: crayon de Jean Calvin," in *Au coeur religieux du XVI⁰ siècle* [Paris, 1957], p. 256).

[13] We will not spend time at this point with those which Calvin maintained with François de Connan, whom he considered to be a highly worthy jurist, and with Nicolas Duchemin, to whom he sent, early in 1537, the work entitled *Comment il faut éviter et fuir les cérémonies et superstitions papales, et de la pure observation de la religion chrétienne* (cf. *Opuscules*, pp. 58-96).

[14] From September 6, 1530, to October 13, 1536, we have ten letters from Calvin to Daniel (nos. 2, 5, 8, 10, 13, 14, 18, 19, 20, and 34 in O.C., X/2; nos. 310, 345, 366, 369, 379, and 380 in Herminjard, II; nos. 437, 438, and 457 in Herminjard, III, and no. 573 in Herminjard, IV), as well as three from Daniel to Calvin between December 27, 1531 and May 15, 1532 (nos. 6, 11, 15 in O.C., X/2, and nos. 362, 375, and 381 in Herminjard, II).

they continued their conversations after having left the university, and even after having taken different sides following the famous placard incident,[15] shows us the warmth of their relationship. Interrupted for many long years, this correspondence commenced again in 1559. Almost thirty years after having been schoolmates, the two friends exchanged a series of letters in which one can read the fidelity and the sensitivity of the Reformer.

The later exchange resulted from the visit of Daniel's second son, who, more consistent than his father, had left Orléans and the "superstitions" in order to find refuge in Geneva, since there he could "serve God purely." Desirous of making peace and reconciling the parents with the runaway, Calvin wrote Daniel: "I beg you not to let loose the bridle of your passion in such a way that you do not judge equitably to find some good that God may have done. . . . But above all I hope that you will be at peace with him. It is not as if he had left like a corrupt and dissipated young man, but since he had zeal to follow God, you would do yourselves a favor by being contented, and I affectionately beg you to be of this mind." [16] This letter did not fail in its intention: François Daniel was moved. He accepted the situation of

[15] Cf. letter of October 13, 1536, sent by Calvin, who was then pastor in Geneva, to Daniel, who, though favoring some reformed ideas, had not as yet broken with the Catholic Church (O.C., X/2, 63-64 and Herminjard, IV, 86-91). This letter is no less friendly than the previous letters from Calvin to Daniel. Abel Lefranc, therefore, is imprecise when he writes: "The difference in viewpoints which showed up after 1534 [the year of the posting of the placards] between the old friends of Orléans days resulted in division and cessation of correspondence" (*La jeunesse de Calvin*, p. 76). The year 1534 did not result in a break between Calvin and Daniel.

[16] Cf. letter of July 15 (according to Baum, Cunitz, and Reuss), or of July 25 (according to Herminjard), 1559, O.C., XVII, 585-86, and Bonnet, II, 285.

his son's remaining in Geneva. And thus by virtue of an old friendship, Calvin directed the studies and provided for the needs of a young student, being concerned for him and offering him advice even after he returned back home.[17]

But during the years spent in Orléans and Bourges, as in Paris, Calvin made some friends not only among his fellow students, but also among his teachers. He developed a friendship with Melchior Wolmar, a Wurtemberger educated in Bern and at Mt. Sainte-Geneviève, who taught him Greek with genuine competence and inexhaustible devotion. After he left Bourges, the future Reformer corresponded with his teacher.[18] Then, doubtless burdened with multiple tasks which overwhelmed him from the time he left France, he neglected Wolmar a little. After five years of silence,[19] sensitive to the reproaches of his old friend who complained of having been forgotten, hoping to make amends he dedicated his *Commentary on II Corinthians* (1546) to Wolmar.

In it Calvin specifically said:

I remember with what affection you have maintained and increased from the beginning the friendship which I have enjoyed with you for such a long time; how often you have been willing

[17] In addition to the letter mentioned above, cf. letters 3138 (*O.C*, XVII), and 3162 (*O.C.*, XVIII sent by Daniel to Calvin, as well as letters 3368 and 3465 (*O.C.*, XVIII) sent by Calvin to Daniel's son after his return to France.

[18] No letter from this period has been preserved. Nevertheless, one can infer from the beginning of the preface to the *Commentary on II Corinthians* ("If you were to accuse me not only of negligence, but also of incivility because it has been so long since I have written a letter: I confess that I would find it very hard to excuse myself" [*Comm., N. T.*, III, 517].) that letters were exchanged for a while between Calvin and Wolmar.

[19] "If I claimed that there are many miles that separate us and that in five full years I have not met one person who was going that way [that is, Tübingen], the excuse would be completely true" (*ibid*).

to give yourself freely, both personally and in influence on my behalf, whenever you thought the occasion presented itself for you to show your love for me; how you offered your influence for my advancement, if the vocation, to which I was then related, should not have prevented me from accepting it. But I have found nothing so good as the remembrance of the first time, when, having been sent by my father to learn civil law, I combined (you being my teacher and master) Greek studies with the study of law. And the Greek studies you taught excellently![20]

The gift which Calvin had of winning the friendship of the other person was not peculiar to his youthful days. In this regard there is no difference between Calvin the student and Calvin the pastor. When he became "minister of the Word of God," he found his friends among his colleagues. It was thus that he developed a friendship with Elie Coraud, an Augustinian, who was won over to the Reformation and became a preacher of the gospel in Geneva. Their work together did not last long because, after having been banished together by the Genevese magistrates, they continued their ministry in different places.[21] But their relationship was so harmonious that the death of the old monk caused a deep sadness to come over Calvin. About this death he wrote to Farel: "I am so staggered that I cannot express how deep my grief is. On that day I could do nothing and was burdened with grief with the same thought all day. The sad anguish of the day was followed by even deeper grief that night."[22]

But the two great friendships which Calvin developed during his first stay in Geneva are those involving the names of

[20] *Ibid.*
[21] As we know, after a brief stay in Basel, Calvin settled in Strasbourg.
[22] Letter of October 24, 1538, O.C., X/2, 273, and Herminjard, V, 166.

Guillaume Farel [23] and Pierre Viret.[24] These two men, in background and age very different—the first was a Dauphinois and almost fifty years old, the second was a Vaudois and not yet thirty—had contributed very much to the introduction of the Reformation in Geneva. The Picard who was the author of the *Institutes of the Christian Religion* had the opportunity of getting to know and appreciate both of them. With Farel, who, aware of Calvin's tremendous abilities, persuaded him to remain in Geneva when he had only meant to pass through, Calvin worked for twenty months to reform the Church according to the Word of God.[25] With Viret, who had preceded him to the side of Farel, he had several meetings[26] before having him as his colleague for ten months[27] on his return to Strasbourg. These relatively brief contacts were sufficient to give birth to an indestructible friendship between Calvin and his two colleagues, whom the mockers, who were jealous of their close relationship, nicknamed "the tripod"[28] and "the three patri-

[23] Cf. the "new biography written by a group of historians from Switzerland, France, and Italy": *Guillaume Farel* (Neuchâtel and Paris, 1930).

[24] The doctoral thesis of Jean Barnaud, *Pierre Viret: sa vie et son oeuvre* (Saint-Amans, 1911), is even today indispensable for a knowledge of the Vaud Reformer.

[25] From the middle of August, 1536, to the end of April, 1538.

[26] Among others, at the Lausanne Discussion in October, 1536, and at the Synod held in the same city in May, 1537, to examine the accusations of Caroli, who unjustly suspected Farel and Calvin of Arianism.

[27] From the middle of September, 1541, to the middle of July, 1542. Cf. Jean Barnaud, *Pierre Viret . . .*, pp. 209-20.

[28] In his *Vie de Calvin*, Nicolas Colladon related: "The people rejoiced in the fine agreement of these three excellent persons every time they saw them together and heard them preach, remembering the first time that they had joined together in Geneva for the leadership of the Church. It is true that there were always some malcontents who were angry at the very presence of Calvin and even more so when they saw

archs." [29] And then when they were separated—when Viret was called to Lausanne, Farel to Neuchâtel, and Calvin to Strasbourg and Geneva—an active and often very moving correspondence maintained their warm unity.[30]

Before emphasizing certain aspects of this correspondence which contradict in a rather formal way the judgment of Imbart de la Tour, according to which Calvin remained "closed and secret, even with his most intimate friends," [31] it is important to point out how the Reformer of Geneva sang the praises of his friendship with Farel and Viret. In the preface of the *Commentary on Titus*, which he dedicated to

---

him in the company of the other two, so that in mockery they spoke among themselves of the union of these three servants of God as "the tripod" (*O.C.*, XXI, 65).

[29] Cf. letter of Viret to Farel, June, 1551: "Multi sunt qui Calvini et utriusque nostrum, quos tres vocant patriarchas, insidientur et detrahere quibuscunque possunt modis conentur" (*O.C.*, XIV, 132).

[30] The wealth of this correspondence is attested to by the number of letters which have been preserved. From Calvin we have 163 letters sent to Farel from August 4, 1538 to May 2, 1564, and 204 letters to Viret written between April 23, 1537 and August 1, or perhaps September 2, 1563 (cf. *O.C.*, XX, 488, n.1). As for the letters which Calvin received from his two friends, they number 322. Of that number, 137, written between August 8, 1538 and August 3, 1562, came from Farel. The other 185 are from Viret, and were written between October 22, 1540 and July 28, 1563.

[31] *Les origines de la Réforme*, IV, 174. August Lang writes in opposition to Imbart de la Tour: "It is moving to observe that the three men were so different in age, personality, and gifts, and yet until the end of their lives they depended on one another; how open they were in their discussions with one another in the smallest and greatest events and in their plans and work, how honest they were also in exposing one another's mutual weaknesses, and how lovingly they shared with one another their smallest and greatest joys and sorrows" ("Das häusliche Leben J. C.," pp. 42-43). Rudolf Schwarz, who, because of his work *Johannes Calvins Lebenswerk in seinen Briefen*, can be considered as the best connoisseur of Calvin's correspondence, expresses the same opinion as Lang (cf. "Calvins Freundschaft," in *Reformierte Kirchen-Zeitung* [Nuremberg, 1909] p. 98).

them in 1549, after having compared their labor in Geneva to that of St. Paul in Crete, he states:

I do not believe that there have ever been such friends who have lived together in such a deep friendship in their everyday style of life in this world as we have in our ministry. I have served here in the office of pastor with you two. There was never any appearance of envy; it seems to me that you two and I were as one person. Then we were separated by many miles. . . . But meanwhile each of us committed himself so well to his respective place that through our unity the children of God assemble themselves as the flock of Jesus Christ, in truth united in his body. . . . And we have shown through visible witness and good authority before men that we have among us no other understanding or friendship than that which has been dedicated to the name of Christ, has been to the present time of profit to his church, and has no other purpose but that all may be one in him with us.[32]

This brotherly fellowship, showing itself in such a beautiful way, is expressed in the correspondence of our threesome not only in the discussion of theological problems and ecclesiastical matters, but also in the total openness in relation to problems of their private lives. It is impossible to note here all the examples of frankness[33] and concern which the

[32] *Comm. N. T.*, IV, 313.

[33] Calvin illustrates this frankness as he chides Farel for his verbosity in his works and in his sermons. On September 1, 1549, he writes to him in relation to a treatise entitled *Glaive de la Parole véritable tiré contre le Bouclier de défense, duquel un Cordelier libertin s'est voulu servir pour approuver ses fausses et damnables opinions:* "I think that the somewhat complicated style and the rather verbose way of approaching the subject only obscure the light which I find in it" (*O.C.*, XIII, 374). Calvin's judgment was justified: the work referred to was no less than 488 pages long and was not even divided into chapters, which might have helped the reading (cf. *Guillaume Farel*, p. 593). As to the length of time Farel was accustomed to use in his

letters exchanged between these three open up for us. However, some features should be related which illustrate the humanness of Calvin.

As everyone knows, Farel was celibate for a long time. A career concerned with preaching the gospel and running here and there wherever his services were needed did not allow him to think of founding a home for many years. Then, when the time came when he needed a lady to clean and keep his house, his colleague in Geneva took care of it. At the end of a letter commenting on the latest news concerning foreign politics and theological publishing, Calvin wrote him: "I am told that you need a maidservant. I do not know of it from you or from the brothers. But since I understand it is spoken of by others, I would like to mention to you that there is a woman here of somewhat advanced age, considered pious and upright and also very neat, who would willingly come to help if she could be useful." [34]

A few years later Farel fell gravely ill. It was believed that he would die. In spite of his many responsibilities Calvin did not hesitate a minute. He immediately set out for Neuchâtel and spent several days at the side of his old friend. The fear he felt of not being able to stand the grief which the death of Farel would bring to him caused him to return to Geneva.[35] But the constitution of the Dauphinois was

---

preaching, Calvin tells us in a letter of January 27, 1552: "From my standpoint there is one thing I want to caution you about: I understand that because of the length of your sermons there are many complaints. You have often confessed that you know this is a fault and that you would like to correct it. Therefore, I ask that you prevent these complaints from growing into seditious clamor, and I beseech you to make a serious effort to restrain yourself rather than giving Satan the chance that we see him looking for" (O.C., XIV, 273).

[34] Letter of February 2, 1550, O.C., XIII, 521.

[35] Louis Aubert does not do full justice to the Genevan Reformer when he says: "Calvin, always in a hurry, left Farel, after having given

stronger than anyone imagined. At the very time when Calvin was saying that he was dead, he recovered. The letter which Calvin sent him at this time reveals what he called "the tenderness of my soul":

After having discharged for your sake what I considered the last duty of a friend, by an early departure I hoped to escape the grief and pain of seeing you die. I have been punished for this haste, and I deserve it. But what is even worse, I have shared my grief with others. However, now revived by such happy news, I forget my folly and my fear (that is, of seeing you die). This great kindness of God dispels every reason for sadness. Having recovered from your illness you must take care to get back your strength of spirit and of body little by little. . . . May it please God, since I have buried you before your time, that the church may see you outlive me.[36]

Five years after having escaped death, Farel suddenly shared with Calvin his intention of getting married. At sixty-nine years the old wrestler, still vigorous, had fallen in love with a young woman from Rouen, Marie Torel, who was a religious refugee in Neuchâtel. One might guess how Calvin received the news of these wedding plans. Believing that his colleague, almost a septuagenarian, might discredit the cause of the Reformation, Calvin told him outright that he would not participate in any way in the engagement or in the wedding,[37] in order not "to give troublemakers a chance to increase their gossip." [38] His viewpoint expressed, he would not give up his friendship. One can see this clearly enough in

him his last goodbyes, to return to his responsibilities" (*Guillaume Farel*, p. 626).

[36] Letter of March 27, 1553, O.C., XIV, 509.

[37] Cf. letter of September 12, 1558, O.C., XVII, 335.

[38] Louis Aubert, *Guillaume Farel*, p. 675.

the letter which he wrote to the pastors of the church of Neuchâtel trying to dissuade them from opposing the wedding of their colleague, as they had given clear intentions of doing.[39] In conclusion he said to them:

I will not stop requesting you to remember how he [Farel] worked for thirty-six long years or more to serve God and to build up the church, how successful his labors have been, and with what zeal he worked, and even the blessings which you have received from him. This should persuade you to have some humaneness—not that you approve of anything bad, but that you not treat him so harshly. However, since it is not up to me to tell you what to do, I will pray that God might guide you into such wisdom and discretion that the incident might be saved from whatever evil results that might possibly be forthcoming, and that the poor brother not be damaged by sadness and gloom.[40]

Contrary to what some writers have believed,[41] Farel's

[39] We cannot agree with the judgment of Louis Aubert, who, observing that the letter of September 12 was "barely half pleasant," considers that here, however, it was a matter of much more than that which concerned Calvin (cf. *Guillaume Farel*, Neuchâtel and Paris, 1930, p. 675). Though Calvin openly expresses his disapproval in relation to Farel's decision he does not fail also to express without reserve the esteem and affection which he has for Farel.

[40] Letter of September 26, 1558, O.C., XVII, 352, and Bonnet, II, 242-43.

[41] T. H. L. Parker writes: "When Farel as an old man married . . . a young girl, Calvin refused to have anything more to do with him," allowing all the same that on his death bed Calvin wrote and forgave his colleague in Neuchâtel (*Portrait of Calvin*, p. 76). Rudolf Schwarz states just as incorrectly: "With this incident the correspondence of these two friends was brought to a sudden end" ("Calvins Freundschaft," p. 100). Between the letters of Calvin to Farel on September 12, 1558 and on May 2, 1564 are found those of October 29 and December 28, 1561 (cf. O.C., XIX, 84-85, 209). As to Farel, after his marriage to Marie Torel, he sent Calvin letters on April 3, 1559, August 9 and

marriage,[42] disapproved of by Calvin, did not break up their friendship nor interrupt the correspondence of the two men. To his colleague in Neuchâtel, Calvin sent his last message on May 2, 1564: "Good health, to you my very good and very dear friend; and since it may please God that you live on after me, please remember our unity, the fruit of which awaits us in heaven, since it has been useful to the church of God. . . . I breathe with the greatest difficulty and expect my breath to fail me at any time. It is enough that I live and die in Christ, who is gain for his own both in life and in death. I commend you to God along with the brothers up there." [43]

Calvin's friendship with Viret was no less rich in moving features than that with Farel. When the reformer in Vaud lost his wife in 1546, Calvin invited him to return to Geneva in order to renew himself. He told him: "Come, in order to deliver your soul from grief and also from cares and concerns. Do not fear that I will give you work to do. So far as I am concerned, you will be allowed to be at your leisure. If someone bothers you, I will intercede. The brothers here make you the same promise as I do. . . . But why am I engaged in slowing you up instead of urging you to hurry on here as soon as possible?" [44]

November 26, 1561, January 11, June 23, July 4, July 9, and August 3, 1562 (cf. O.C., XVII, 493-94; XVIII, 601-2; XIX, 137-38, 248-50, 468-69, 484, 491-93). These letters, whether Farel's or Calvin's, contain nothing contrary to the rules of good friendship.

[42] It took place in Neuchâtel on December 20, 1558.

[43] The French translation of this Latin letter (cf. O.C., XX, 302-3) is found in the eulogy of Théodore de Bèze (O.C., XXI, 44) and in the biography of Nicolas Colladon (O.C., XXI, 103).

[44] Letter of March 8, 1546, O.C., XII, 305. In translating this passage, Jules Bonnet (as is his habit) allows himself unpardonable liberty. But sadder yet, in order to add to the pathos, in a single quotation he blends the most moving passages from Calvin's two letters—one from

If he shared the griefs of his friends, Calvin also knew how to relate himself to their joys. When Viret remarried and then became a father to several children,[45] his friend in Geneva did not fail to find the mood suitable to his fresh happiness. In order to be convinced of this, one need only read the letter sent by Calvin to the pastor in Lausanne inviting him to a party in the country:

If you intend on coming, I beg you to come to our house on Saturday. You would never find a better time all this year. Sunday morning you will preach here in the city and I will leave for Jussy. You may join me there after lunch. From there the two of us will go to M. de Falais' home.[46] From his place we will move on to the other side where we will remain in the country at the homes of Lisle and Pommier [47] until Thursday. On Friday if you wish to make a trip to Tournay or to Bellerive, you will also have me for a companion. . . . Try not to miss all this, much awaits you here. Until you come, goodbye. Greet the brethren and also your wife and little girls.[48]

It is important to note that without being touched up these lines can only show us the depth of a friendship which delights the perspective of one who observes it. They also blast the legend of a sad Calvin, who was a stranger to all that brings sweetness and charm to life.

The friendship Calvin had with Farel and Viret did not exhaust his affectionate resources. During his three years in Strasbourg,[49] the time between his banishment from Geneva

February 22, before the death of Viret's wife (cf. O.C., XII, 296) and one from March 8, 1546 (cf. *Récits du XVI* siècle*, 1, 155-56).

[45] Cf. Jean Barnaud, *Pierre Viret*, p. 318.

[46] In Veigy, between Jussy and Hermance.

[47] Probably in Cologny.

[48] Letter of July 23, 1550, O.C., XIII, 603.

[49] From the beginning of September, 1538, to the end of September, 1541.

and his return to Geneva, he developed a friendship with
Martin Bucer, with whom he had previously corresponded [50]
and because of whom he had settled down in Alsace.[51] This
is not the place to relate all that Calvin owed to Bucer in
the area of theology.[52] It is not useless, on the other hand,
to quote the sentences in which the French Reformer encouraged his Strasbourg colleague, who was forced in 1549
to find refuge in England, leaving behind a wife and children,
because he was not willing to subscribe to the Augsburg
Interim, by means of which Charles V promoted the restora-
tion of Catholicism in Protestant territory:

Ah! If I could only relieve you some from the grief in your
soul and the anxieties which I know must torment you! We all
pray for you that you have not been allowed to suffer this blow

[50] Cf. the first letter of Calvin to Bucer: no. 16 in *O.C.*, X/2, 22-
24, and no. 477 in Herminjard, III, 202-4. Baum, Cunitz, and Reuss,
following Doumergue, date it September 4, 1532. Herminjard and
Lefranc date it September 4, 1534, and Lang and Walker are inclined
to place it later than 1534 (cf. Williston Walker, *Jean Calvin: L'Homme
et l'oeuvre*, trans. E. and N. Weiss [Geneva, 1909], pp. 73-74). Without
desiring to settle the question here, we believe that the date of 1532
is unlikely, agreeing with François Wendel (cf. *Calvin: Sources et
évolution de sa pensée religieuse* [Paris, 1950], p. 20). By the tone of
familiarity in this letter, we know that Bucer was no stranger to Calvin.
Therefore, it must have been preceded by a more or less extensive
exchange of letters between the two men.
[51] We know that Bucer, as Farel had done in Geneva in 1536, had
urged Calvin in the name of God to perform his ministry in Strasbourg.
In his preface to the *Commentary on the Psalms*, Calvin comments on
this subject: "I had decided to live in solitude without taking a public
post until the fine servant of Jesus Christ, Martin Bucer, using a similar
argument to that employed by Farel earlier, called me to another
position. Being rather terrified by the example of Jonah which he
suggested to me, I again entered the office of teaching" (*Comm. Ps.*,
I, 9).
[52] On this subject, cf. chap. 6, "L'influence de la pensée de Bucer
sur la pensée de Calvin," Jaques Courvoisier, *La notion d'Eglise chez
Bucer dan son développement historique* (Paris, 1933), pp. 135-50.

unavailingly. Not that we desire to see you happy and content since you have many diverse reasons to be sorrowful. This is not what is required of you, this is not what we hope for you. Insofar as is possible, you must strive only to set yourself apart for the Lord and for the Church.[53]

Besides Bucer, two very worthy men were well known by Calvin in Strasbourg:[54] Jean Sturm, founder of the Haute Ecole, and Jean Sleidan, a diplomat whose *l'Histoire de l'état de le religion et république sous l'empereur Charles V* [55] was authoritative for several centuries. And also from this period dates a most amazing friendship which Calvin nurtured the rest of his life—a friendship with Philip Melanchthon,[56] whom he met at the Frankfort Conference (1539) and saw again at the Colloquies in Worms (1540-41) and Ratisbon (1541).[57] Though the French Reformer and the Preceptor

[53] Letter 1297, O.C., XIII, 437 (the date is unknown, but can be fixed with probable certainty in October, 1549).

[54] Our list does not attempt to be exhaustive. During the Strasbourg period a friendship occurred with Claude Féray, deacon in the French church. At his death Calvin wrote Farel: "It is unbelievable how overcome with grief I am as a result of the death of my Claude. But this should not be surprising to you. You can imagine what a loyal and faithful friend he has been during these two years—he has supported me so much in the midst of numerous and diverse irritations and difficulties" (Letter of March 29, 1541, O.C., XI, 175, and Herminjard, VII, 56).

[55] Title of the French translation, which appeared in 1557, of the work entitled *De statu religionis et reipublicae, Carolo quinto Caesare, Commentarii* (1555).

[56] To the point Léopold Monod writes: "Perhaps nowhere else are the regard and sensitivity of Calvin's friendships accentuated in such a moving way as in his relationship with Melanchthon. If it were not rather childish to try to set up a hierarchy of values in such a matter, I would strongly believe that Melanchthon was the man to whom Calvin was most sensitively related. . . ." (*Le caractére de Calvin*, p. 13).

[57] Calvin gave public testimony to his friendship with Melanchthon in dedicating to him, in February, 1543, his *Réponse aux calomnies*

of Germany (as he was often called) had a similar humanistic background in common,[58] on the other hand, they had different personalities and theological positions. Calvin stuck to the theological positions which appeared foundational to him (he was not called "the theologian"[59] without good cause), while Melanchthon was more inclined to compromise positions. Calvin was committed to a strong insistence on the doctrine of predestination while Melanchthon was led progressively away from this viewpoint.[60] Despite different temperaments and these divergent doctrinal positions, the two men remained good friends throughout their lives.

If such loyalty deserves to be remembered, it must be clearly emphasized that the gentleness of Melanchthon was not the only reason for it. Calvin also helped to create and sustain this friendship, first of all by his breadth of viewpoints. In 1546, Calvin translated the *Loci theologici*, the dogmatic work in which the Wittenberg theologian set forth his thought, and which, on more than one point, disagreed with Calvin's own thought. He did even more than translate

---

d'Albert Pighius contenant la défense de la sainte doctrine contre le franc arbitre des papistes. In the preface to this work, Calvin states: "I feel sure that for two reasons you will be pleased with this book which I dedicate to you: that is, because you like the author of the book, and then because it concerns itself with defending a holy and sound doctrine, which you not only hold in high esteem, but which you also defend most excellently and constantly" (*Opuscules*, p. 257).

[58] A background which, as François Wendel has so ably put it, "created a kind of complicity of intellectuals between them" (*Calvin: Sources et évolution* . . . , p. 40).

[59] Cf. *Joannis Calvini vita*, by Théodore de Bèze, O.C., XXI, 130.

[60] Emile Doumergue writes the following in relation to these evolutions in opposite directions: "Little by little Melanchthon abandoned the doctrine of predestination, dating from the second edition of the *Loci* (1535), just as Calvin, to the contrary, committed himself to it with increasing strictness from the second edition of his *Institutes* (1539)" (*Jean Calvin* . . . , II, 545).

it: he wrote a eulogistic preface for the translation. With this
openness of spirit he combined patience. Without growing
weary and without allowing the silence of his correspondent
to be discouraging to him,[61] with a tactful frankness he urged
him to fear dangerous concessions, and, after Luther's death,
to take up the responsibilities which fell upon him. Finally,
if this friendship endured in spite of numerous and dangerous
reefs, it was because of a mutual affection, whose depth one
can measure by means of the words of regret spoken by the
Genevan Reformer one year after the death of his friend in
Wittenberg:

> Oh, Philip Melanchthon! I call you now as a witness before
> God with Christ, we wish that we might be reunited with you
> in that wonderful resting place. You told me at least a hundred
> times, you were weary of work and even overwhelmed with so
> much ennui when you laid your head familiarly on my breast:
> "Would to God, would to God that I might die today with my
> head upon this bosom!" And as for me, I have wished a thousand
> times that we might be together again.[62]

Returning to Geneva in September, 1541, Calvin remained
there the rest of his life. In spite of the difficulties which he
encountered there, and in spite of the battles which he had

[61] The *Opera Calvini* contain 13 letters from Calvin to Melanchthon
between February 16, 1543 and November 19, 1558, and 8 letters from
Melanchthon to Calvin between February 11, 1540 to October 8,
1557.

[62] It is at the beginning of his treatise against the ultra-Lutheran
theologian Tilemann Hesshus, entitled *Déclaration naïve de la saine
doctrine de la vraie participation de la chair et du sang de Jésus-Christ
en la sainte-cène* (1561), that Calvin thus calls forth the memory of
Melanchthon, who agreed with his ideas about the eucharist (*Opuscules*,
p. 1694).

to wage there for some fifteen years,[63] he never withdrew into himself. He made many friends there, especially among the refugees who flooded into the city. As if his friendship needed to reach out beyond the theological environment, he related well to a number of laymen of noble background, who had given up privileges, and, at times, even wives and children in order to be able to confess their faith openly:[64] Jacques de Falais, a great-grandson of Philip the Good, duke of Burgundy, who had been promoted to the court of Charles V; Laurent de Normandie,[65] one of the king's lieutenants and mayor of Noyon; Guillaume de Trie,[66] nobleman of Varennes; Galéas Caracciolo,[67] marquis de Vico and nephew of Paul

[63] With the end of the "perpetual alliance" between Geneva and Bern in January, 1558, the opposition to Calvin was definitely muzzled.

[64] We do not list them in the order of their arrival in Geneva.

[65] Calvin, who was a fellow native of Noyon and who had studied law at the same time he did at the University of Orléans, dedicated his *Traité des scandales* to him. After having praised the steadfastness of Laurent, who, following his arrival in Geneva, had lost in succession his father, his wife, and his daughter, Calvin wrote in his preface: "I also intend this little book to testify to the love which I have for you to those who know you. I know that you do not need such a pledge, for you are convinced of my love. There are several bonds which tie us closely together: there is no familial relationship nor acquaintance which surpasses our friendship" (*Opuscules*, p. 1147, and *Trois traités*, p. 153).

[66] His death in 1561 called forth some very moving words from Calvin. Cf. letter to Théodore de Bèze, August 27, 1561, O.C., XVIII, 649-50.

[67] To Caracciolo, who separated himself from his own relatives so that he might not have to give up the Reformed faith, Calvin dedicated the second edition (1556) of his *Commentary on I Corinthians* (the first edition was dedicated to Jacques de Falais whose name was "scratched" because of the sympathy he had shown for Bolsec). After having referred to the wonderful loyalty of the Marquis de Vico, Calvin stated in his preface: "Though I am trying here to set forth your virtues as in a mirror for the eyes of the readers so that they might be pleased to imitate and follow them, it would be a shame for me, who sees them and knows them so much better, if I were not moved by them to be lively in my faith as I contemplate them so clearly every day. However,

IV; and finally Charles de Jonvillers, who became his devoted secretary.

His friendship with Jacques de Falais, which was terribly strained when Falais sided with Bolsec against Calvin, illustrates how zealous and how sensitive Calvin could be toward his friends. For several years, until Falais settled down in Geneva, the two men carried on an active correspondence.[68] First, the Reformer invited him to take the road of exile for loyalty to the gospel. Then, when he had convinced him to come and live in Geneva, he spent time in finding a house for him. Having found one, he took charge of making the repairs on it, clipping the vines in the garden, gathering the grapes, purchasing a cask of good wine, and procuring a wood pile, pending the arrival of the new owner. But Calvin's interest was not limited to material matters. Eager to defend Falais from the accusations which had been directed against him following his adoption of the Reformation, Calvin found time to write an apology on his behalf which was destined to be presented to the emperor.[69]

---

for my part, no matter how much your example results in the strengthening of my own faith and belief in God, . . . it would seem that it is good for me to set it forth carefully that this witness might be similarly useful to those who are far from here" (*Comm. N. T.*, III, 270).

[68] We have 46 letters from Calvin to Jacques de Falais, written between October 14, 1543 and 1552 (cf. the last letter, O.C., XIV, 448-50 and Bonnet, I, 363-66), and 7 letters sent to Madame de Falais by Calvin from October 14, 1543 to November 20, 1546. On the other hand, none of the letters sent to Calvin by Jacques de Falais are preserved.

[69] This apology, entitled *Excuse de noble Seigneur Jacques de Bourgogne, Seigneur de Falais et de Bredam, pour se purger vers la Majesté impériale des calomnies à lui imposées en matière de sa foi, dont il rend confession* (1547), was only known to the editors Baum, Cunitz, and Reuss in the Latin translation done by François Baudoin (cf. O.C., X/1, 269-92). The French text by Calvin was discovered in Geneva and published in Paris in 1896 by Alfred Cartier.

Friend

If Calvin made friends with some of the faithful laymen who had been forced out of their homeland and had come to the church of Geneva to increase their faith, he also found among the groups of refugees some colleagues who were very dear to him: Nicolas des Gallars, Michel Cop, brother of the former rector of the University of Paris, and Nicolas Colladon. But perhaps the one to whom he felt closest was Théodore de Bèze, ten years his junior, whom he had doubtless met along with Melchior Wolmar when he studied at Bourges,[70] and who, after 1558, would be his brilliant successor in Geneva. Nothing illustrates Calvin's affection for Bèze better than the letter which he wrote to a French friend during a sickness of his young colleague (however, the friendship was developed much earlier than their collaboration):

When your messenger came to me bearing your letter to Bèze, I was hit with a fresh fear and, at the same time, overwhelmed with deep sorrow. Actually, yesterday someone told me that he had been stricken with the plague. So I was not simply worried about the grave danger he was in. Staggered, so to speak, I was already weeping for him—I love him so much—as if he were already dead. My grief did not arise as much from my love for him as from my general concern for the church. Of course, I would be inhuman if I did not love him for my own part—for he loves me more than a brother and respects me as a father. But I still grieved more for the loss there would be for the church if, through sudden death, we would have taken from us at the beginning of his career a man from whom I expect so many great things. . . . I hope that our prayers for his continued life will be granted.[71]

[70] Cf. the remarkable biography by Paul-F. Geisendorf, *Théodore de Bèze* (Geneva and Paris, 1949), p. 11.

[71] Letter of June 30, 1551, O.C., XIV, 144-45. As we see, Calvin's friendship, deep as it was, was subordinated to his more important

Bèze recovered, and some six years later, had the chance to prove, in a rather delicate situation, the strength of the friendship Calvin felt for him. Sent with Farel to plead before some German princes the cause of the Vaudois of the Piedmont, who were threatened by the king of France, Bèze encountered in Germany some Lutheran theologians, with whom he discussed the thorny question of the Lord's Supper.[72] At their request he drafted a confession of faith concerning the Eucharist in which, for the sake of irenicism, he made some concessions.[73] The pastors in German Switzerland, upset over the use which some supporters of an exacerbated confessionalism made of this confession, did not miss the chance, by means of their representative Bullinger, to lodge a protest in Geneva against the author. Calvin, so critical in doctrinal matters, did not disown Théodore de Bèze. He replied to Zwingli's successor as follows: "Since there is nothing dangerous in Bèze's confession, I willingly excuse him for having shown moderation in love for his brothers and for trying to calm angry men." [74] Dissatisfied with this answer, Bullinger renewed his charge. But Calvin did not change his answer: other than admitting that Bèze had not been too clear, he defended him to the end.[75]

---

interest in the church. Rudolf Schwarz correctly states: "He loved his friends and he held them in high regard. If any trouble came to them, he was not frightened away, and, for this reason, friendship for him was never self-serving. But, so far as he was concerned, no friend should evade his lifework on his account; moreover, friendship should never interfere with God and his kingdom" ("Calvins Freundschaft," p. 133).

[72] Concerning this matter, cf. Aubert, *Guillaume Farel*, pp. 658-61, and Geisendorf, *Théodore de Bèze*, pp. 83-88.

[73] Cf. the text of this confession, dated May 14, 1557, in *O.C.*, XVI, 470-72. Louis Aubert gives a slightly shortened French translation in *Guillaume Farel*, p. 659.

[74] Letter of August 7, 1557, XVI, 565.

[75] Cf. letters of August 31 and October 13, 1557, *O.C.*, XVI, 595-96, 666-67.

Friend

Other illustrations could be given. They would show just like all those we have given that Calvin was not the isolated hero nor the lonely genius that he has often been pictured. Throughout his career, he had relationships with friends who showed him unfailing affection and indefatigable devotion. If he exerted such charm, it is certainly because he himself had been such an incomparable friend. To the affection which one brought to him, he responded with an unfailing love. For the devotion which one showed for him, he paid the tribute of unswerving loyalty.

Chapter 3
Pastor[1]

Calvin was a pastor for some twenty-seven years. During this period, which is exactly one-half his whole life, he was a minister in Geneva, then in Strasbourg, and finally he returned to his first parish, where he remained until his death. Few pastors have had as fertile a ministry as he had. Few persons have made as deep a mark in history as he did. In order to describe in one phrase this ministry which ran far beyond ordinary dimensions, one can do no better than to refer to the judgment of Emile G. Léonard, according to which

[1] On this subject cf. Paul Martin, *Un directeur spirituel au XVI*[e] *siècle: Etude sur la correspondance de Calvin* (Montauban, 1886); Emile Doumergue, *Jean Calvin* . . . , II, 67-84, 407-27, 666-68; V, 113-25; Eugène Choisy, "L'éducation des consciences et la doctrine de Calvin," in *Calvin, éducateur des consciences* (Neuilly-sur-Seine, 1926), pp. 39-59; Wilhelm Kolfhaus, *Die Seelsorge Johannes Calvins* (Neukirchen Kreis Moers, 1941); Jean-Daniel Benoit, *Calvin, directeur d'âmes* (Strasbourg, 1947); Edmond Grin, "Calvin pasteur," in *Revue de théologie et de philosophie* (Lausanne, 1949), pp. 202-5; Erwin Mülhaupt, *Reformatoren als Erzieher* (Neukirchen Kreis Moers, 1956), pp. 51-71; Pfisterer, *Calvins Wirken in Genf*, pp. 115-33; and Cadier, *Calvin, l'homme que Dieu a dompté*, pp. 107-34.

Calvin "invented a new kind of man in Geneva—Reformation man—and in him sketched out what was to become modern civilization." [2]

In the face of the magnitude of such a work, which is still the basis of so much theological endeavor, and which composes fifty-nine volumes[3] without even counting the unpublished works which are being published presently,[4] one tends to stress the exceptional side of the Reformer and to forget the character traits which we will describe next. In this section our aim is to give several illustrations from Calvin's ministry which show his humanness. First, they will reveal for us his attitude in relation to several events of decisive importance, and then they will show us his conduct toward the faithful to whom he ministered.

The Reformers who were banned from Geneva in April, 1538, left behind a group of persons who favored them and who organized together the most zealous members of the church under the name of "Guillermins." [5] It would have been easy for Calvin to encourage them not to recognize their new pastors (some of whom were monks who had recently come over to the Reformation position), for some of them were not really equal to the task. Far from becoming bitter, which would have been understandable, Calvin refrained from maintaining a resistance force in the midst of his former

[2] *Histoire générale du protestantisme*, I: *La Réformation* (Paris, 1961), p. 307.

[3] *Ioannis Calvini opera quae supersunt omnia*, ed. Baum, Cunitz and Reuss (Brunswick and Berlin), 1863-1900.

[4] This concerns the unpublished sermons being published under the title *Supplementa calviniana* by Neukirchen Kreis Moers. The first volume, *Predigten über das 2. Buch Samuelis* was edited by professor Hanns Rückert and appeared in 1961.

[5] This nickname was used for "Guillaumins" and came from Farel's first name, Guillaume.

flock. On October 1, 1538, renewing contact with the faithful in Geneva (after several months of no contact), he wrote them a letter [6] in which, rather than posing as head of the group, he asserted himself only as a true member of the church.[7] Without making explicit allusion to the events which had caused his departure, he invited his correspondents to consider the recent vicissitudes as a test designed to correct their nonchalance, increase their zeal, and strengthen their faith.

A bit later, Calvin took another step. One of the warmest of his Genevan partisans[8] asked him whether it was right to receive the Lord's Supper from the new ministers. Calvin did not hesitate to answer in the affirmative. And to justify his position he wrote to Farel (who did not share his viewpoint) the following:

There must be among Christians such a hate for schism that they will avoid it as strongly as they can. It is necessary that there be such a respect for the ministry and the sacraments that anywhere men see them existing, they must also consider that there is the church. Therefore, whenever, in the providence of God, it happens that the church is directed by men such as those in Geneva, if Christians can perceive in the situation the marks of the church, it is preferable that they not separate themselves from her communion. It is not an obstacle if certain impure doctrine is taught there: almost no church exists which does not have some trace of ignorance. It suffices for us that the doctrine

[6] Cf. O.C., X, 251-55, Herminjard, V, 121-26 and Bonnet, I, 11-18.

[7] This judgment follows Amédée Roget's description of the style of this letter of October 1, 1538: "Here is certainly the language of a member of the church and not of the head of a party" (Histoire du peuple de Genève, I, 133).

[8] Antoine Saunier, rector of the college.

which constitutes the foundation of the church of Christ may have and keep its place.[9]

Calvin's conciliatory attitude did not disarm the opposition of the Guillermins against the new preachers, who, concerning themselves more in retorting than in preaching the gospel, did not succeed in maintaining the work of their predecessors. It was necessary for this to end, however, at the risk of dangerously compromising the Reformation. Encouraged by Calvin, who was detained in Strasbourg due to responsibilities in his parish, Farel made peace with the new ministers in Geneva,[10] who admitted their wrongs toward the reformers. This reconciliation which occurred among the pastors did not immediately find fruition among the Guillermins. They continued to look at their spiritual leaders as usurpers. Animated only by a desire for unity, Calvin again addressed himself to his former parishioners who were so attached to him personally.

He wrote them as follows:

Dearly beloved friends, nothing has saddened me any more, since the troubles which have so terribly dissipated and nearly overthrown your church, than to learn of your differences and disputes with the ministers who followed us there. Although the irregularity which led to their installation and which remains even now may have with good reason, given you offense, I can only hear with a great and deep horror that there is a schism in the church which you are causing. . . . But now when I learn, contrary to what I hoped for, that this reconciliation between your

[9] Letter of October 24, 1538, O.C., X, 275 and Herminjard, V, 169.
[10] This reconciliation, which took place on March 12, 1539, in Morges under the auspices of the Bernese preachers, is called the "Concord of Morges." Cf. *Guillaume Farel*, p. 43.

pastors and the neighboring churches, a reconciliation effected by Farel in person and approved by me, has not been able to unite you, by reason of a feeling of sincere friendship and by right of a genuine relationship, I feel that I am obligated to write concerning you to your pastors, to whom is entrusted the care of your souls, in order to try as hard as I can to find a solution for this terrible problem.[11]

What was the solution? Calvin tells us a few lines later:

I only hope that towards those who in a certain way perform the office of pastor, in whatever ways they are supportable, you will conduct yourselves as Christians and that you will occupy yourselves more in doing to others as you would have them do to you.[12]

A little more than a year after this letter that was so completely inspired by love of peace and harmony was sent, the Genevan authorities, dissatisfied with the work of their pastors,[13] took steps to get Calvin to return. In their view he was the only one capable of straightening out a dangerously compromised situation. Happy in Strasbourg, Calvin really had no desire to return to Geneva. He had openly said to Farel that he preferred "a hundred deaths to this cross." [14] After having been disgracefully chased out of his first parish, he could rightfully have rejected in a haughty manner this appeal addressed to him to resume his ministry in Geneva. But Calvin was not the kind of man who held a grudge

[11] Letter of June 25, 1539, O.C., X, 351-52 and Herminjard, V, 336-38.

[12] Ibid.

[13] During the summer of 1540, two of them, "Jean Morand and Antoine Marcourt, quit their jobs and left town without asking permission" (Walker, *Jean Calvin: l'homme et l'oeuvre*, p. 279).

[14] Letter of March 29, 1540, O.C., XI, 30 and Herminjard, VI, p. 199.

when the interest of the gospel was involved. It suffices to quote from the letters to the Genevan syndics to show the feelings which motivated him. He wrote in his letter of October 23, 1540, as follows:

With God as my witness I tell you that I hold your church in such high regard that I would never want to fail its needs in anything that I could do. And now I do not doubt that it may be terribly distressed and in danger of being further weakened unless it has its needs supplied. And because of this I am in a terrible quandry, desiring to answer your request and trying with every ounce of grace God has given me to make the best decision.[15]

Several weeks later he added:

I assure you that in every way that it will be possible for me to use to meet the needs of your church I will do my duty, as if I had already accepted the call which you extended me; indeed, almost as if I were already among you laboring as a pastor. This concern which I have that your church be well supported and governed would never allow me not to try every means possible to me in helping to meet her need.[16]

After having complied with the advice of his friends, and of Farel in particular, and having sacrificed his personal preference to the cause of the Reformation, Calvin returned to Geneva on September 13, 1541. Several days later[17] he was in his pulpit. What a wonderful chance to recall the past errors and to preach what is called a "situation-in-life sermon"! However, here, too, the Reformer does something different

---

[15] O.C., XI, 95-96, Herminjard, VI, 333, and Bonnet, I, 30.

[16] Letter of November 12, 1540, O.C., XI, 105, Herminjard, VI, 354, and Bonnet, I, 34. Cf. also the letter of February 19, 1541, O.C., XI, 158-59, Herminjard, VII, pp. 28-29 and Bonnet, I, pp. 36-38.

[17] Probably Sunday, September 18. Cf. Herminjard, VII, 412, n. 20.

from what one might have expected. He relates the following to an unknown correspondent:

> When I came before the people to preach, everyone was eaten up with curiosity. But, remaining completely silent about the events which surely they all expected me to mention, I set forth very briefly the principles of my ministry, and then quickly and discreetly I recalled to mind the faith and the integrity of those who supported me. After this introduction I began to comment on the text at the place where I had stopped (at the time of my banishment). By doing this I wanted to show that rather than having given up the teaching office, I had only been interrupted for awhile.[18]

The magnanimity illustrated by such words was enforced by a tireless patience and used in the interests of unity. Never forget the fact that on the question of the Lord's Supper the reformers had different viewpoints. Feeling these differences more painfully than many others, Calvin, supported by Farel, engaged himself from 1540 on[19] in negotiations with Henry Bullinger in Zürich with a view to reaching some agreement with the Zwinglians. After nine years of laborious discussions and reciprocal concessions, a ground of agreement was found. In 1549 a conclusion between Calvin (who had agreed on the banks of the Limmat) and the successors of

[18] Letter 384, O.C., XI, 365-6; letter 1090, Herminjard, VII, 412. This letter, which probably dates from the end of January, 1542, was sent to Sébastien Münster, professor of Hebrew in Basel according to Herminjard (cf. p. 413, n. 26).

[19] Cf. André Bouvier, *Henri Bullinger, le successeur de Zwingli, d'après sa correspondance avec les réformés et les humanistes de langue française* (Neuchâtel and Paris, 1940), p. 125. One may refer to this work (pp. 125-44) for a history of the steps taken by Calvin with the Zürichers in order to arrive at a common accord concerning the Eucharist.

Zwingli was reached in the *Consensus tigurinus*.[20] This was also accepted by the churches in Bern and Basel and formed the doctrinal unity of Helvetic protestantism.

It was not theological reasons only that motivated Calvin in this matter; it was also pastoral instability. To perceive this one only needs to refer to the letter which he sent to his colleagues in Zürich by way of introducing the text of their agreement: "I have already told you several times that some persons were offended because it seemed to them that we, you and I, did not completely agree with one another in our teaching. And I could not see a better method of doing away with this scandal than by working together privately to find a good means to show and to prove the agreement that exists between us. So not long ago, as you know, I made a trip to your city." And in order to justify the publication of the articles of the *Consensus*, he added: "In truth we can certainly say that we experienced harmony between us. But even though I simply do not have to persuade you about everything in it, it would be unfortunate if those for whom I desire some peace on this subject were left in suspense and doubt. . . . For this reason I think that there is no more suitable thing to do in follow-up than to give public testimony of what we have agreed on among ourselves." [21]

Thus, having contributed to the agreement of the Swiss churches on this subject, Calvin then turned to Luther's followers in hopes of rallying them to the cause of Protestant unity.[22] His efforts never had the success he hoped for.

[20] O.C., VII, 733-48; French translation in *Opuscules*, pp. 1138-43 and in *Calvin, homme d'Eglise*, pp. 133-42.

[21] *Opuscules*, pp. 1137-38 and *Calvin, homme d'Eglise*, pp. 132-33.

[22] Wendel correctly describes the relations of Calvin with the Lutherans of Germany when he writes: "If he did not always understand them and if they did not always understand him, certainly it was not

The Humanness of John Calvin

Dragged into a sterile polemical controversy with Joachim Westphal, an ultra-Lutheran theologian from Hamburg who attacked the Zürich Accord, he was never able to make contact with those in Germany who were not so opposed to his views.

An event, which is not well known, should be mentioned at this point which illustrates both the suspicion which many Lutherans had in relation to the Genevan Reformer as well as the breadth of spirit which vivified Calvin. In 1556, at the height of his controversy with Westphal, he went to Frankfort-on-the-Main in order to arbitrate a conflict which was dividing the French church. The City Council [23] requested that the German language pastors have discussions with him. They refused, alleging that they were not able to answer him.[24] Even though there was peril in having such a meeting, Calvin engaged in conversation with his Lutheran colleagues. He told them that in inviting them to a discussion he had had no other motive than the search for unity, and he added that he would not open a discussion against their wishes. Finally,

---

a question of the purity of his motives" (*Calvin: Sources et évolution* . . . . p. 70).

[23] To this Council, in 1555, Calvin dedicated his *Commentaire sur l'Harmonie évangélique* because of the welcome it was giving to religious refugees. In his dedication Calvin states: "Not only have you maintained among you the pure service of God, and carefully given orders that your subjects keep themselves peacefully within Christ's flock; but also the relics and scattered remnants of the dispersion of the church who have been chased out and torn in many directions—they are gathered and the pieces are put together by you again" (*Comm. N. T.,* I, 11).

[24] Concerning this refusal, the Lutheran theologian Mülhaupt writes: "Do we not clearly have this impression: one avoids Calvin therefore only because one worries that the very human, pleasant, and winning nature of this man might confuse one in one's own point of view, which, indeed, one is not willing in any case to give up?" (*Reformatoren als Erzieher,* p. 57).

being directly exposed to what he had to say, they were so greatly amazed that one of them would have acclaimed him as a divine appearance as a result of his style of speaking to them.[25] Even in his openness to dialogue and his kindness, the Reformer from Geneva failed to convince his interlocutors! [26]

Some years later, after these unfruitful discussions, at the time when the religious wars were brewing in France, Calvin showed his horror of violence and his aversion to fanaticism (another characteristic of his pastoral attitude). Thus, he condemned the conspiracy of Amboise (1560), which the Protestant party had developed, with its goal being the overthrow of Francis II and the removal of the Catholic influence of the Guise family.[27] Likewise he warned the Reformed churches in his homeland, which were growing stronger every day, against the temptation of seizing Catholic churches in

[25] Cf. letter from Calvin to Wolfgang Musculus, October 26, 1556, O.C., XVI, 319-20.

[26] On the "ecumenical" efforts of Calvin, cf. Willem Nijenhuis, *Calvinus oecumenicus: Calvijn en de eenheid der kerk in het licht van zijn briefwisseling* ('S-Gravenhage, 1958), as well as John T. McNeill, "Calvin as an Ecumenical Churchman," in *Church History* (1963), pp. 379-91, and *Unitive Protestantism* (Richmond, 2nd ed., 1964), pp. 178-220.

[27] Cf. letter to Admiral de Coligny, April 16, 1561, in Bonnet, O.C., XVIII, 425-31 and Bonnet, II, 382-91. Calvin states there in relation to the conspirators: "I have said openly that if their folly succeeded, I would be the most degraded man on earth, as having betrayed the church, having impeded the work of God, having opposed liberty, and things like that" (O.C., XVIII, 429-30, and Bonnet, II, 388). Despite such reservations, Henri Naef, an expert on this subject, assumes the innocence of Calvin (cf. *La conjuration d'Amboise et Genève* [Geneva, 1921], pp. 159-63). Even if, as Naef believes, without ever bringing out any final proof, Calvin had "in the depths of his soul . . . a hope of unexpected success" (*ibid.*, p. 163), he had never encouraged nor favored the Amboise conspiracy.

order to use them for their worship services.[28] He warned them of the danger of wanting to respond to force by the use of force.[29] However, when trouble broke out in the Midi, agitated by certain Protestants with the concurrence or the instigation of their pastors, his indignation hit the limit.[30]

To the church in Sauve,[31] which allowed itself to be swept along in an iconoclastic fury under the direction of the minister Tartas, Calvin wrote as follows:

If everyone practiced the rule which the Holy Spirit gave us from the mouth of St. Paul, to conduct oneself prudently and in all modesty, . . . you would not be in such distress . . . and we would not be troubled to judge you and to urge you to remedy the scandal which is already present and to see that such deeds do not happen in the future. We hear of the foolish things being done in Sauve, of the burning of images and the destruction of a cross. We are amazed that there has been such temerity

[28] Cf., for example, the letters to the Paris church (February 26, 1561) and the Montpellier church (August, 1561), O.C., XVIII, 376-78, 661-62, and Bonnet, II, 378-82, 418-20. We read in the first: "Of scattering out too much and occupying the churches, you know that this has never been our advice, except by permission. When this has been done, we have had contempt. If it continues, we will leave the matter in God's hand. We fear that this heat may not cool off in such a harsh storm" (O.C., XVIII, 378 and Bonnet, II, 381).

[29] Cf. among others, the letters to the churches of Valence and Montélimar, April, 1560, and the one to the church of Aix, May 1, 1561 (O.C., XVIII, 63-64, 64-66, 432-37 and Bonnet, II, 330-32, 332-36, 392-94). In the first, Calvin writes: "You must strengthen yourselves not to resist the rage of the enemies by means of fleshly arms, but you must thereby hold up the truth of the gospel in which our salvation consists as well as the service and honor of God, which we must value more than our bodies and our souls" (O.C., XVIII, 63 and Bonnet, II, 331).

[30] Cf. the note "Calvin et les briseurs d'images," in BSHPF (1865), pp. 127-31.

[31] In the present state of Gard.

among those who should have restrained the others and kept them
bridled.

And, responding to the objection of the pastor in Sauve who
pretended that he had acted in good conscience, Calvin
added: "Though he tries to delude us by saying there is
proof that it is based on the Word of God, we know the
contrary to be true. God has never commanded such a destruction of images, except to each man in his own home and
in public to those he has given authority." [32]

In no less energetic terms Calvin disapproved of the ex-
cesses committed in Lyon in 1562. Exasperated by the news
of the Vassy massacre, Protestants in Lyons had seized control
of the city and had pillaged the Church of St. John. At the
end of a letter sent to their ministers in which he denounced
the scandal bred by such acts, Calvin said quite bluntly:
"We cannot talk to you sweetly about these matters and we
cannot hear about them without deep shame and bitterness
of heart. Now as late as it may be to remedy it, though we
cannot do it, we must beg you in God's name and exhort
you as much as we can to take great pains to atone for your
past sins and, above all, to forsake your robbing and pillaging.
It would be better to forsake such persons who are the in-
stigators of disorder and to be separate from them rather than
expose the gospel to such disgrace by having anything to do
with them." [33] As one can see from these examples, and

[32] Undated letter, but probably dating from June or July, 1561,
O.C., XVIII, 580-81 and Bonnet, II, 416-17.
[33] Letter of May 13, 1562, O.C., XIX, 410, and Bonnet, II, 467.
Cf. also the letter of the same day sent to the Baron of Adrets, O.C.,
XIX, 412-13, and Bonnet, II, 468-70, in which Calvin speaks against the
old soldiers who intend "to loot the chalices, reliquaries, and other
items in the churches," and against the pastors, who, falling in with

contrary to certain legends, Calvin was not a wild type of person or one who tried to stir up the passions of men.

If in the unusual events in his ministry Calvin gives proof of having qualities which set in relief a humanness which is often ignored, how did he conduct himself in ordinary and daily affairs? How did he act in his relationships with his parishioners or with his numerous correspondents? He acted in such a way that one can see in his concern for souls the secret of his patience.[34] Jean-Daniel Benoit says: "One loves to speak of him as the Reformer of Geneva. It would perhaps be more correct to refer to him as the pastor of Geneva, because Calvin was a pastor in his soul, and his reformatory work, in a good many respects, was only the consequence and extension of his pastoral activity." [35]

The correspondence allows us to gaze at a picture of Calvin in private conversation, if we can say it this way, with his flock. It is an infinitely less harsh picture than the legendary one! At this point we will exhibit only two characteristics from the picture:[36] first, the trait of complete devotion and several examples will be sufficient as illustrations. In 1538, when the Reformer was in Basel, he learned that the nephew of Farel had been stricken with the plague. Without fear of danger and thinking only of his responsibility, he went to the bedside of the sick boy in order to take the comfort and encouragement of the gospel, he took care of his expenses, and when he died, Calvin took care of the expenses

---

these deeds of pillage, disgracefully endanger "the cause which is so good and so holy in itself" (O.C., XIX, 412, and Bonnet, II, 469-70).

[34] Cf. Pfisterer, *Calvins Wirken in Genf*, p. 19, repeated by Kolfhaus, *Die Seelsorge Johannes Calvins*, pp. 9-10.

[35] *Calvin, directeur d'ames*, p. 18.

[36] For a complete picture one is referred to the works cited earlier of Kolfhaus and Benoit which show in an excellent way the qualities of Calvin as pastor and as guide of his parishioners' consciences.

for the burial.[37] A few years later, after returning to Geneva, he intervened in order to get a poverty-stricken individual hospitalized. He wrote the director of the hospital as follows: "Since it is such a pitiful case, would you please see if there is some way to help him so that he might not die. I commend him to you all the more strongly since I believe that he may be from Geneva. If he were a foreigner, I would consider looking after him some way myself." [38] At the death of Guillaume de Trie, taken from his family in the prime of life (1561), Calvin accepted the responsibility of the guardianship of the orphans. In view of this heavy task which fell to his lot, he stated to Théodore de Bèze: "I owe it to the memory of my wonderful friend to love his children as if they were my own. . . . It would be a criminal act if I were to break the trust which has been placed upon me.[39]

As to the devotion of Calvin, one must also relate a whole series of humble services, wearisome tasks sometimes, but those which reveal the character of a pastor. He requests Viret to find lodging in Geneva for an old woman who was not successful in acclimatizing herself in Strasbourg where

[37] Cf. letter to Farel, August 20, 1538, O.C., X/2, 235-37, and Herminjard, V, 86-89. It must be pointed out at this juncture that Calvin, contrary to the statements of some historians, did not fail in his responsibilities during the plague of 1543. If the Genevan authorities did not consider him at that time to be one of the possible chaplains for the hospital, it is certainly because they believed it terribly dangerous to expose him to the disease, since he played such an important role in the church and in the city. In case he should have been appointed to be the chaplain to those stricken with the disease, he would not have refused this formidable task as is proved by his letter to Viret at the end of October, 1542 (cf. O.C., XI, 457-60 and Herminjard, VIII, 163-76). On this question also cf. Doumergue, *Jean Calvin* . . . III, 147-50 and Pfisterer, *Calvins Wirken in Genf*, pp. 119-25.

[38] Letter of 1542 or 1543, O.C., XI, 482 and Herminjard, VIII, 236-37.

[39] Letter of February 11, 1562, O.C., XIX, 285.

she was a refugee.[40] He asks Myconius, Oecolampadius' successor in Basel, to find a family there with whom the son of one of his parishioners might live in order to learn German.[41] He addresses the same request to Bullinger on behalf of four young men whom the Genevan authorities decided to send to Zürich at Geneva's expense.[42] He offers to find an apprentice's place with a painter in Geneva for the nephew of a colleague in Neuchâtel.[43] He requests Renée de France to procure a dowry for the daughter of François Porto, long-standing professor of Greek at the University of Ferrara.[44] For a nobleman who is a refugee, he drafts a letter which the young man sends to his father who is opposed to the Reformation.[45] He sets himself to the task of finding a woman of pleasing appearance and an easy-going personality for a young man who wants to get married.[46] Many are the ex-

[40] Cf. letter of August 13, 1541, O.C., XI, 261-63 and Herminjard, VII, 216-19.

[41] Cf. letter of May 1, 1546, O.C., XII, 343-44.

[42] Cf. letter of September 6, 1560, O.C., XVIII, 176-77. Cf. also the end of the letter of October 1, 1560, O.C., XVIII, 208, in which Calvin requests lodging for a certain Michel Planchon, whose father was one of Calvin's friends.

[43] Cf. letter to Farel, October 24, 1555, O.C., XV, 841-42.

[44] Cf. letter of May 10, 1563, O.C., XX, 15-18, and Bonnet, II, 513-16.

[45] Cf. O.C., XIV, 542-44, and Bonnet, I, 387-90. In this letter, Calvin has the nobleman, whose commitment to the faith causes him to disobey his father, to say to his father the following: "Since God has given me grace to decide what is good or bad, it is necessary that I decide for myself using this standard" (O.C., XIV, 543 and Bonnet, I, 389). From this statement it is not really proper that Kampschulte accuses the reformer of having claimed infallibility for himself (cf. *Johann Calvin: seine Kirche und sein Staat in Genf*, I, 276). The German historian has not even observed that in this letter it is not Calvin who is supposed to be writing, but rather the young viscount of Aubeterre. Cf. Doumergue, *Calomnies anti-protestantes* (Paris and Lausanne, 1912), I, 111-14.

[46] Cf. letter to Farel, July 1, 1558, O.C., XVII, 227-28.

amples from the pastoral ministry which have no extraordinary qualities about them; they are commonplace. But it is surprising to discover them in the life of a man whose job was overwhelming and whose responsibility was considerable.

Devotion is not the only unknown characteristic of Calvin's pastorate. Inseparable from his psysiognomy is a second trait which should be mentioned, one which shows that he was not the unfeeling calculator, cold intellectual, and uncompromising leader whom men have painted in the legend. As amazing as it may sound, the Reformer had been blessed with the gift of sympathy, capable of being developed into genuine compassion. He wrote to Viret whose child had had to be weaned because of another pregnancy of the mother: "I can sympathize with the pain of the little girl. But when a brother or a sister is given to her she will forget the hurt which her mother has given her. I hope that she has already escaped from the major pains of the weaning." [47] He writes to Madame de Grammont, whose husband had cheated on her: "I well know what anguish you have, seeing that your partner continues to be disloyal to you. . . . However, pray to God daily that he may change your husband's heart and, in your own way, try to win him back and set him on the right road. I know how difficult this is for you since you have already been betrayed several times. . . . But you must still work on it this way since it is the best remedy." [48] He consoled and encouraged a father who had lost his little boy before the child had been baptized. He reminded him of the promise: "I am the God of your children." He instructed him that "we have our names in the book of life . . . by the good

[47] Letter of July 6, 1549, O.C., XIII, 319.
[48] Letter of October 28, 1559, O.C., XVII, 661, and Bonnet, II, 292-93.

grace of our God." [49] He attended the wife of Laurent de Normandie in her last hours, and, having been given the responsibility of telling the father in France of the death of the young refugee, he told Madame de Cany, who would transmit the sad news: "Speaking of love, St. Paul never forgets that it is fitting for us to weep with those who weep; that is, if we are Christian, we must have such compassion and sympathy for our neighbors that we would freely bear part of their grief in order to ease them somewhat." [50]

But the most touching letter which Calvin wrote is the one which he sent to M. de Richebourg when his son, who had boarded in Calvin's home in Strasbourg, was swept away by the plague during the time Calvin was at the Ratisbon Colloquy. The Reformer wrote as follows to the grief-stricken father:

When the news first reached me of the death of Master Claude [Féray] and your son Louis, I found myself so distracted and confused in spirit that for several days I could do nothing but cry. And in prayer to God I was not comforted at all nor helped by the aid which he gives us in times of adversity, however, in the presence of people it seemed to me that I had control of myself. . . . On the other hand I was seized by grief and pain that such a young man, who had so many wonderful potentialities, as did your son, had been taken away from us—carried off in the very beginning of the prime of his life: you see that I loved him as if he were my own son, and he honored me as if I might have been his second father.

After thus having expressed his grief, Calvin added as an introduction to his consolation:

[49] Letter of September 6, 1554, O.C., XV, 228, and Bonnet, I, 438.
[50] Letter of April 29, 1549, O.C., XIII, 247, and Bonnet, I, 300.

But I am telling you all this so that the remonstrances and admonitions with which I now want to console you will not be a heavy burden for you if by chance it would seem to you that it is easy for me to be steadfast and brave when it is a matter of someone else's grief. And, in fact, I am not urging my steadfastness in the grief of another here, but rather saying that God in his unique goodness has given grace to deliver me in some way or to alleviate the grief and pain which I have in common with you, almost in the same degree as you. I decided to write you, as much as a letter and a brief letter at that can share, the remedies which I have tried and have found to be of great help to me in the midst of such trouble. How well I know that in such a situation I must have great respect for the sadness which you must feel; I remind myself that I am writing to a serious person, mature in prudence and gifted with great steadfastness.[51]

As moving as it was, this letter should not allow us to forget the role which Calvin played in relation to the faithful Protestants and the Protestant communities in France which were persecuted because of their faith. He never stopped advising them, encouraging them, sending them pastors, and showing them a sympathy of which one hears an echo in these words addressed to the brothers in the church in Paris: "Now there is really no need as yet to declare formally that if you are experiencing perplexity and anguish due to the dangers which are so close by, we feel it also among ourselves. For we think you know us well enough to be convinced that we are not so thoughtless as to forget those with whom we are joined in brotherly bonds in faith and who even battle for the cause of our salvation. But difficulties beset us more and more, so much so that there is nothing we can

---

[51] Letter probably dating from early in April, 1541, O.C., XI, 188-90, and Herminjard, VII, 66-68. Jules Bonnet was unaware of the existence of this letter.

do to help you; there is nothing for us except to grieve in compassion." [52]

It is in his attitude toward captives and martyrs that the Reformer shows the full measure of his humanness.[53] Without hiding his compassion for them, and without sparing his efforts to deliver them whenever he could, he knew how to prepare them for the specious interrogation of the inquisitors, to strengthen them during their distressing detention, and to assure them of celestial blessing in view of the danger of a horrible death. So he corresponded with Richard Le Fèvre[54] before LeFèvre was put to death at the stake, and told him that he was going to the wedding feast of the Son of God along with Matthieu Dimonet,[55] who died "joyously and praying to the Lord"; with Denis Peloquin and Louis de Marsac,[56] whose heroic steadfastness before the flames aroused the pity of the crowd; with Madame de Rentigny[57] and with Madame

[52] Letter of June 29, 1559, O.C., XVII, 575, and Bonnet, II, 282.

[53] Kolfhaus and Benoit agree in recognizing this moving side of the ministry of Calvin as a witness to the faith. The former writes: "A very big part of his time and his warmest love was extended to the imprisoned and to the companions in the faith who were threatened with death. As a result of his deep concern for them, he sent encouragement and consolation, very often even up to their last hours" (Die Seelsorge Johannes Calvins, p. 88). The latter states: "Calvin was a pastor and counselor for martyrs! This is one light in which he is too little known. However, perhaps this facet of his career reveals the genuine depth of his life and is the clearest illustration of his piety" (Calvin . . . , p. 61).

[54] Cf. letter of January 19, 1551, O.C., XIV, 19-24, and Bonnet, I, 316-25.

[55] Cf. letter of January 10, 1553, O.C., XIV, pp. 467-69 and Bonnet, I, 367-71.

[56] Cf. letters of July 7 and August 22, 1553, O.C., XIV 561-64, 593-96 and Bonnet, I, 395-99, 399-404. According to Jean Crespin's l'Histoire des martyrs, the first of these letters was also sent to Matthieu Dimonet.

[57] Cf. letter of December 8, 1557, O.C., XVI, 726-29, and Bonnet, II, 159-63. In a second letter, dated April 10, 1558, O.C., XVII, 131-

de Longemeau,[58] who were both imprisoned after the St. Jacques Street affair in Paris. Avoiding the double reef of mawkish sentiment and illusory piety, he did not urge them to be soft with themselves and he never hid from them the gravity of their situation. In a very strong way he shared their suffering. He always said to all of them in one way or another what he wrote to one who was imprisoned who remains unknown to us: "Since the cause for which you are suffering is common to all of God's children, we want to be participants in your suffering insofar as we are able; however, since we have no other means of fulfilling our responsibility except to pray to God in our prayers of the compassion and concern which we have for you, please be aware that we never fail to do this." [59]

This tone is found not only in the letters he sent to individuals, but also in those he sent to groups of prisoners. Nothing is more touching than his correspondence with the "students" in Lyon.[60] They were five young Frenchmen, who, after having taken theological studies under Viret and Bèze in Lausanne, returned to their homeland, where they acted out their missionary zeal only to be arrested and sentenced to die. Just

---

32 and Bonnet, II, 189-92, Calvin asks Madame de Rentigny to pull herself together again, who, at the request of her husband, appeared on the verge of recanting in prison.

[58] Cf. letter of December 14, 1557, O.C., XVI, 734-35 and Bonnet, II, 169-71.

[59] Letter of November 13, 1559, O.C. XVII, 669, and Bonnet, II, 307.

[60] Cf. letter of June 10, 1552, O.C., XIV, 331-34 and Bonnet, I, 340-45; two undated letters, unknown to Bonnet, O.C., XIV, 423-25, 469-71; letter of March 7, 1553, O.C., XIV, 491-92, and Bonnet, I, 371-74; and an undated letter, O.C., XIV, 544-47, and Bonnet, I, 382-86.

as moving are his messages to prisoners in Chambéry,[61] five pastors, themselves also French, who left Geneva to preach the gospel and were taken prisoner in Savoy and handed over to the executioner. Finally, also very touching were his letters to men[62] and women[63] prisoners in Paris, who, guilty of gathering together to celebrate the Lord's Supper, saw several of their number taken away to the stake. One must read this correspondence in order to understand the kind of encouragement it must have brought to those to whom it was sent.[64] It brought encouragement in the certainty that God acts and is present even in the darkest dungeon and bright hope concerning eternal life; it helped to make victors of those whom adversity had intended to conquer.[65]

Such a man was Calvin in the carrying-out of his ministry: a pastor whose distinguished qualities made a deep impression

[61] Cf. letter of September 5, 1555, according to Bonnet (O.C., XV, 707-9, and Bonnet, II, 63-66) and letter of October 8, 1555 (O.C., XV, 809, and Bonnet, II, 77-79.) Also cf. Bonnet, *Récits du XVIe siècle*, II, 39-76.

[62] Cf. undated letter (probably September, 1557), O.C., XVI, 632-34 and Bonnet, II, 145-49.

[63] Cf. letter of February 15 (and not February 18 as Bonnet says), 1559, O.C., XVII, 436-39, and Bonnet, II, 253-57.

[64] We will give only one example. Before their death, the Chambéry prisoners sent a message to Calvin. It begins with these words: "Master and very esteemed father in our Lord, we received your letters of September 5 and they have helped us greatly. For they are a testimony to us of the strong love which you and your brothers have for us. But you sympathize so deeply with us in the evil which comes to us in the flesh that you may not allow yourself to rejoice with us in the blessings which come to our spirits—weeping with those who weep and laughing with those who laugh. We thank you for all this very warmly" (O.C., XV, 805-6).

[65] *L'Histoire des martyrs* by Jean Crespin (cf. edition by Daniel Benoit and Matthieu Lelièvre, 3 vols. [Toulouse, 1885-1889]), shows on every page the great spirit which the first martyrs of the Reformation displayed before their death.

on his contemporaries who knew him best. Nicolas des Gallars, who was his colleague in Geneva for several years, summed up Calvin's pastoral ministry in these words:

What labors, what sleeplessness and worry he bore, with what keenness and finesse he forsaw dangers, with what zeal he guarded against them, what fidelity and understanding he showed in everything, what a kind and obliging spirit he had toward those who came to him, how quickly and frankly he answered those who asked him even the most serious questions, with what wisdom he settled both privately and publicly the difficulties and problems which were posed for him to settle, with what sensitivity he comforted those who grieved and lifted up the broken and discouraged, how resolutely he opposed the enemies, how ardently he attacked the prideful and the obstinate, with what grandeur of spirit he endured misfortune, with what restraint he behaved in prosperity, and finally with what dexterity and élan he discharged all the duties and responsibilities of a true and faithful servant of God, I could certainly not be able to convey fully by the use of any words.[66]

---

[66] Latin preface to Calvin's *Commentaire sur le prophète Esaïe*, sent to the editor, Jean Crespin, in 1570, O.C., XXXVI, 15-16.

Conclusion

When Calvin is viewed in the context of his roles as husband and father, as friend, and finally as pastor, he shows up as one endowed with a rich and full humanness. However, it would be a mistake to idealize him. To decorate his picture with some sort of halo would actually be to wrong him. Because he had his weaknesses and his faults, his limitations and his gaps. He knew his needs better than anyone. And, also, before his death did he not try to admit this for the sake of posterity? In true humility,[1] which is one of the secrets of his greatness, he saw himself as he really was during his career and asked for forgiveness from those whom he had offended.

Taking his resignation to the Syndics and to the members of the Council of Geneva on April 27, 1564, he thanked them for having been willing to "support him in several situations when he really needed it"; he requested them "to accept the

[1] Cf. Pierre Marcel, "L'humilité d'après Calvin," in *La Revue Réformée*, Saint-Germain-en-Lay, 1960, no. 2, pp. 33-8.

good intention instead of the result" if he had not done everything that he should have done; he requested that they pardon him for "having done so little compared to what he should have accomplished both publicly and privately"; he expressed his appreciation to them for having "supported him in his terribly strong feelings." [2] Giving a farewell speech to his tearful ministerial colleagues the next day, he said to them: "I have had many faults that you have had to endure, and all that I have done is of no value. The vicious person will hear this statement happily; but I still say that nothing I have done is really worth much and that I am a wretched and sinful creature. Though I can say that I have had a good motive and will to do the right, my defects and faults have always given me offense, and that the roots of the fear of God have been in my heart. You can say that the affection has been proper and good. I beg you, that the evil be forgiven me." [3]

Finally, in his testament,[4] setting before God the balance sheet of his life, the Reformer confessed:

He has had mercy on me, his poor creature, . . . to draw me to the brightness of his gospel and to make me a sharer in the doctrine of salvation, of which I was so unworthy, . . . he has put up with me even in the midst of faults and weaknesses which really deserved rejection a thousand times by him. But what is more, he extended his mercy to me until then I served him and labored for him in order to set forth and proclaim the truth of

[2] Farewell address to members of the Small Council, in *O.C.*, IX, 887-88; Bonnet, II, 569 and *O.S.*, II, 398. Nicolas Colladon gives the slightly different account of the secretary of the Council in his *Vie de Calvin* (cf. *O.C.*, XXI, 99-101).

[3] Farewell address to the ministers, in *O.C.*, IX, 893, Bonnet, II, 576 and *O.S.*, II, 402.

[4] Chronologically this testament is prior to the last meetings which Calvin had with the representatives of the civil authorities and with the Genevan pastors. Its date is April 25, 1564.

his gospel. . . . Alas! the desire and the zeal which I had, if one can call it that, have been so cold and so lax that I feel endebted in all things and all places, and, if it were not for his great and infinite kindness, all the affection that I have had would be only smoke. To see the good things that he has done for me only makes me more guilty, so that my only recourse is to that One who, being the Father of mercy, may be and show Himself to be the Father of one who is such a wretched sinner.[5]

"Such a wretched sinner!" Is not this confession the best proof that Calvin was not the inhuman or anti-human person whom some people have believed him to be? After having offered "his heart as a burnt sacrifice to the Lord," [6] after having spent body and soul for the triumph of the gospel, far from shutting himself up in a prideful contemplation of his sacrifice or of his genius, he felt a solidarity with sinful humanity which can find justification only in Jesus Christ.

[5] O.C., XX, 299, and Bonnet, II, 564. The testament is found: (1) In the eulogy written by Théodore de Bèze in 1564 immediately after Calvin's death (cf. O.C., XXI, 42), (2) in the biography by Nicolas Colladon, 1565 (cf. O.C., XXI, 98), and (3) in the Vie de Calvin, written in Latin and published by Théodore de Bèze in 1575 (cf. O.C., XXI, 162-64).

[6] Answering Farel, who was urging him to return to Geneva, Calvin wrote on October 24, 1540: "If I had the choice, I would rather do anything than to comply with your wishes in this matter. But when I remember that I am not my own, I offer my heart as a burnt sacrifice to the Lord" (O.C., XI, 100, and Herminjard, VI, 339). In these latter words we see the slogan of the Reformer and the commentary on his seal: a heart resting on the palm of a hand (cf. Ernst Pfisterer, Calvins Wirken in Genf, p. 114).